COVENT GARDEN PAST

First published 1995
by Historical Publications Ltd
32 Ellington Street, London N7 8PL
(Tel: 0171-607 1628)

ISBN 0 94866727 3
British Library Cataloguing-in-Publication Data
A catalogue record for this book is available from the British Library.

Typeset in Palatino by Historical Publications Ltd
Reproduction by G & J Graphics, London EC2
Printed in Zaragoza, Spain by Edelvives

COVENT GARDEN
PAST

John Richardson

HISTORICAL PUBLICATIONS

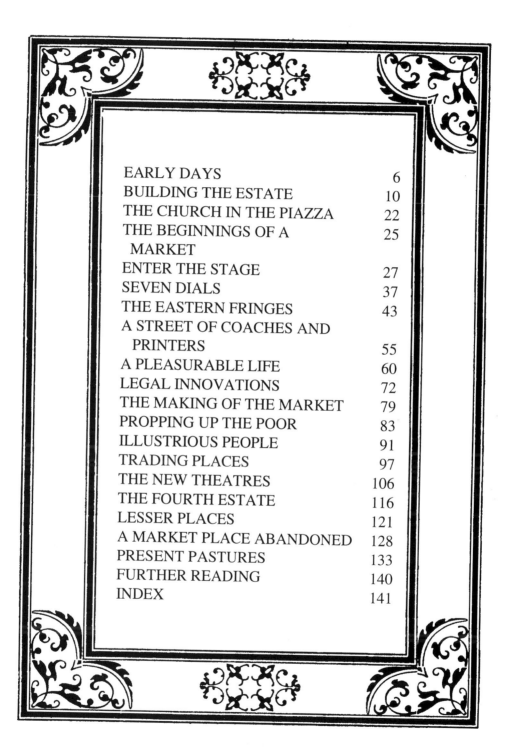

1. *The 'Agas' bird's-eye map of London c1560. To the bottom left, above the entrance to Whitehall, is Charing Cross, set up by Edward I to commemorate his queen, Eleanor. Houses line both sides of the Strand, though they are larger on the river side. The convent garden belonging to Westminster Abbey may be seen in the centre of the picture, with Drury Lane to the east going up to High Holborn and leading to St Giles-in-the-Fields. At its southern end Drury Lane forks to a narrow alley that went on down to the Strand, and to a wider road, Wych Street; at this junction stands Drury House, erected in the reign of Elizabeth I.*

Early Days

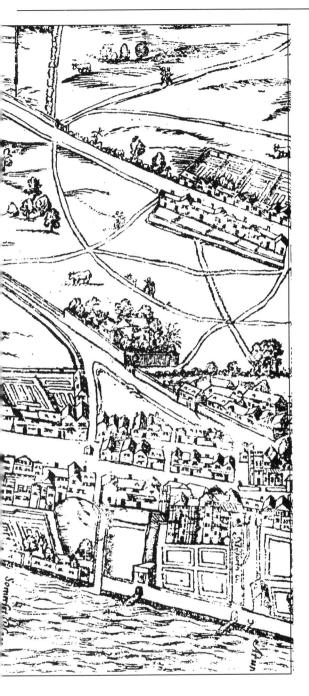

A SAXON SETTLEMENT

Histories of Covent Garden have usually begun with the existence of a medieval convent garden belonging to the abbey of St Peter, Westminster (Westminster Abbey), but recent discoveries extend the area's story back into Saxon times. It is now thought that two hundred years after the abandonment of the City of London by the Romans in AD410, a new settlement, called *Lundenwic*, was established by Saxons outside the City walls, along Fleet Street and the Strand, spreading northwards through what became Covent Garden.

Our knowledge of the London area in the immediate post-Roman period is threadbare and feeds on remarkably few bits of archaeological information. So little has been found in or beyond the City walls that it is still unclear if London was inhabited in any significant way in the two centuries following the Romans' precipitate retreat. Given that the Roman *Londinium* was in effect the prosperous capital of the British province, it is extraordinary that so little is known about it and for so long a period. What happened to the indigenous, British, population of the City during that period is a puzzle and, presumably, there were settlers and traders in London as well as Romans who for whatever reason did not need to obey the call back to Rome.

The Romans as conquerors were superseded by the Saxons from Germany and northern Europe, who, on the evidence available at present, do not appear to have settled behind London's fortified walls. Not only are there no meaningful archaeological reminders of them within the City in the first two hundred years after the Romans left, but no Saxon cemeteries have been found within eight miles of London.

Theories abound to account for this apparent recklessness. One is that there was plague in the City, another that the Saxons felt uncomfortable within walls and preferred open countryside – other Roman cities in England were neglected by them. However, this lack of evidence is not hard evidence and given the destruction of archaeological sites in the Victorian and post-Second World War periods, it is still too early to be dogmatic about the matter. What we do know is that when London surfaces again, early in the seventh century, its administration was entirely different to that imposed by the Romans, revolving around king and bishop, a duality of power located in the north-west of the City around the Roman Cripplegate fort and the newly founded St Paul's. Furthermore, the Saxon road pattern was different from that of the Romans, other than in the area of that same north-west section.

By 601, London was of sufficient importance again, or else its Roman status had lingered on, for Pope Gregory to nominate it as the principal see of England. In the event, for political reasons, Canterbury secured that honour and London became a bishopric instead.

It was during excavations in Covent Garden in the 1980s that a breakthrough was made in our knowledge of the spread of London in the seventh and eighth centuries. Finds on the site of the old Jubilee Hall, in Bedfordbury, Maiden Lane, Shorts Gardens, and further north in Great Newport Street and Trafalgar Square, indicate that a substantial Saxon settlement existed on the gravel bank which stretched from the river Fleet at Ludgate Circus to the bend of the Thames at Charing Cross.

These discoveries have led to the proposal that the Saxons established a port called *Lundenwic* along the Thames here – the Strand was its shoreline, with the river much wider then – supported by a small town on the higher ground of what is now Covent Garden. (There is in fact quite a steep slope from the river to the Piazza, as a walk from behind the Savoy Hotel and up Southampton Street will confirm.) Aldwych – a name first encountered in 1211 – is thought to mean 'old port'. If this suggestion is correct then the description by Bede in *c*731 of 'a metropolis.... a mart of many peoples coming by land and sea' at last makes sense, for no evidence of a mart in the walled area of the City at that time has so far been discovered.

Little or nothing has been found to suggest that the Saxons settled in the Covent Garden area before the seventh century and *Lundenwic* seems to have been created just at the time when London within its walls was beginning to stir out of its post-Roman slumber.

No doubt more will be found as and when excavation is possible, though the achievement in recent years of saving Covent Garden from redevelopment has severely reduced opportunities for archaeologists.

In later medieval documents 'Aldwych' is used to denote the length of Drury Lane, which may perhaps have been the north-south extent of the settlement. It is also suspected, but not yet proved, that the line of churches along Fleet Street and the Strand, from St Bride's to St Martin-in-the Fields, is a vestige of a string of Saxon foundations.

Nothing later than the mid-Saxon period has so far been discovered in Covent Garden, almost certainly because the ferocity and frequency of Viking raids made it necessary for the Saxons to retreat behind the City walls. To no avail, however, for many were slaughtered in London in 842, and the City was again sacked in 851.

CHANGES OF OWNERSHIP

Most likely the area which made up *Lundenwic* came into the ownership of the Benedictine Abbey of St Peter, Westminster, in *c*969. The actual convent garden, some forty acres, is first documented in about 1200 and was, during the thirteenth and fourteenth centuries, a mixture of orchard, meadow and arable, yielding barley, apples, pears, plums and other produce which found its way to the dining tables of the monks at Westminster. Roughly, the garden lay between St Martin's Lane and Drury Lane on west and east, and north and south between Floral Street and Maiden Lane. It may be seen clearly in Hogenburg's map of London, surveyed in about 1550, behind the buildings then lining the Strand, and in the so-called 'Agas' map of about ten years later, reproduced here. The convent also owned two adjacent pieces of land in the area of the Strand Palace Hotel, Exeter and Southampton Streets, called Friars Pyes, and to the north of the convent garden, seven acres collectively called Long Acre. The monks kept the garden under their own care until about 1407, and then let it out.

Henry VIII snapped the land up in 1536 when the abbey was obliged to exchange this potentially valuable tract for an estate in Berkshire. The bargain, of course, was unequal, but monastic houses had to shift as best they could at the time, and by 1540 Friars Pyes had also gone into the royal portfolio.

By grants of 1541 and 1552 the estate came into the hands of John Russell, the first earl of Bedford, thus beginning a landlord and tenant relationship that was to last four hundred years. Russell served Henry VIII both as a soldier and a diplomat and was rewarded with a large number of titles and estates. Even though subsequent times were treacherous for those with misplaced allegiances, the Bedford family was to grow in influence and affluence under successive monarchs and even today still owns large swathes of Bloomsbury directly to the north of Covent Garden. Many of London's street names derive from their estates such as those at Tavistock and Woburn.

The importance of the transfer of substantial London estates at the time of the Dissolution from the monasteries to lay hands, via the acquisitive conduit of the Crown, cannot be overstated. In the seventeenth and eighteenth centuries the new owners took a more commercial view of land development than their old ecclesiastical owners would have managed. Because of this the expansion of London was fairly unfettered and suburbs of London were built, as needed, in a succession of squares and fine adjacent streets.

John Russell did not live on his Covent Garden estate – his mansion was across the road on the south side of the Strand, a thoroughfare that then had fashionable status. The Strand connected the two

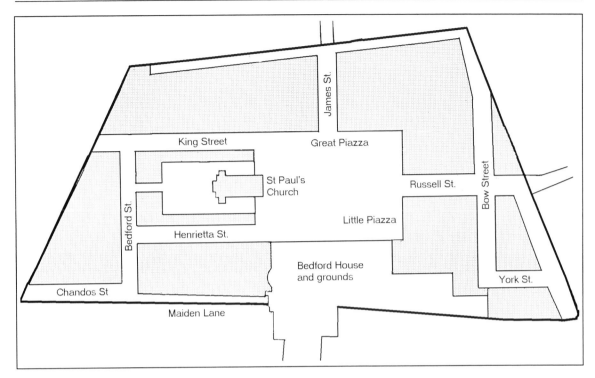

2. Plan of the inner Covent Garden estate, within the wall built by the third Earl of Bedford by 1613.

cultures of London – the commercial City and governmental Westminster, with legal Fleet Street nearby. A number of wealthy courtiers had houses on the south side of the Strand, as not only were there river views as the Thames swept round at right angles at Charing Cross, but there was immediate access to water transport from their own rear gardens.

The third earl, Edward Russell, built a new family home on the Covent Garden estate. It stood facing the Strand (where Southampton Street now lies) and by 1613 he had also built a wall which surrounded twenty acres of the old convent garden, the line of which is indicated in Illustration 2. The southern wall marked the south side of Maiden Lane, until it encountered the grounds of Bedford House. On the east side of the grounds it continued as far as today's Catherine Street, then north to the east end of Floral Street, then west and then in a south-westerly diagonal down to Chandos Street. It was in this twenty acres that the first planned suburb of London was later built. The relatively spacious inner Covent Garden streets, King, Bedford, Russell and Henrietta Streets, represent the old area inside that wall, and contrast with the less planned, usually narrower roads and alleyways outside the enclave.

It was Edward Russell, too, who began the commercial development of the northern part of the estate. In conjunction with the Mercers' Company, a lessee of some of the land, he laid out what is now Long Acre – the Mercers' saintly insignia may still be seen on a number of buildings in this area.

For the purposes of this book we have included as part of Covent Garden the areas adjoining the Bedford estate which in time housed businesses and occupations intimately associated with those of Covent Garden, particularly, of course, those of the market. Thus, the estate developed by the Mercers' Company north of Long Acre and the scheme of roads radiating from Seven Dials planned by Thomas Neale are included. So too is that neighbourhood to the east around Great Queen Street which, before the blunt creation of Kingsway, was more logically associated with Lincoln's Inn Fields.

It was the predominance and expansion of the market which physically, and in perception, enlarged the extent of Covent Garden so that when, in the 1960s, planners turned their attentions to the area, they included all the streets between Kingsway and Monmouth Street/St Martin's Lane, and between High Holborn and the Strand.

3. *Covent Garden Piazza and St Paul's church, by Sutton Nicholls, 1717-28, looking north. No.43 King Street (built c.1717) is
just beyond the portico of the church, already disturbing the symmetry of the arcaded houses, one of which it displaced. A pillar has
been erected in the square, and the railed-off area is the equivalent of the eventual market place. At this stage the market occupies
only the southern part of the square, with a few semi-permanent sheds. Four steps led from the portico of the church (unclear in
this print) to the Piazza – today the church is at ground level, an indication of how the level of the Piazza has been raised since.*

Building the Estate

PROHIBITION

The Covent Garden estate was developed at a time when there were prohibitions on building in London and Westminster. Alarmed by the rapid growth of the metropolis, Queen Elizabeth in 1550 forbade the erection of new houses within three miles of the City, and James I allowed building only by licence, and only then in brick and stone. It was both a form of building control and a source of revenue to the Crown which appealed to his son, Charles I who, in his disputatious relationship with Parliament, was perpetually short of money.

How Covent Garden came to be built and the extent of the involvement of the architect, Inigo Jones, are matters still in some obscurity. Sir John Summerson has pointed out that the building of the estate stemmed from a fortunate conjunction of three talented men: 'Charles I, with his fine taste and would-be autocratic control of London's architecture; [Inigo] Jones with his perfectly mature understanding of Italian design; and the [4th] Earl of Bedford with his business-like aptitude for speculative building'.

Charles I, like his father before him, had architectural ambitions for his capital and was conscious that London, despite its fine array of churches and palaces, was less resplendent, less monumental than other cities in Europe. Even when Charles was insecure on his throne during the Civil War that followed, he still pursued a magnificent scheme to transform his straggling palace at Whitehall into something that would be envied abroad. All that got built was the Banqueting House, which still survives in Whitehall.

Francis Russell, the fourth Earl of Bedford (1593-1641) was reputed to be greedy and uncultured. He was however, as Summerson noted, a business man and had already shown his acumen by organising a successful draining of fenland in East Anglia, and in rebuilding Woburn Abbey. It was not surprising that he should devote his energies to the development of a London estate most likely to bring in revenue. Unusually in a peer whose fortunes derived from the Crown, he leant in sympathy toward those in Parliament who discomfited the King, but his acquisition of a licence to build, even for a fee of a much-needed £2,000, implies that there is still much to learn about the Earl's relationship with Charles.

There is also much to know about the involvement of Inigo Jones. There is no document in the Bedford archives that indicates him working on the scheme, and yet we know from other sources that he designed the church of St Paul and, probably, the houses on the north and east side of the Piazza. Jones, responsible more than any other for the popularisation of classical

4. Charles I, from a painting by Daniel Mytens, 1631.

5. Inigo Jones.

architecture at that time in England, had been appointed Surveyor of the King's Works by 1620 and was also a member of a commission whose duties included the enforcement of the very building prohibitions that the Earl of Bedford was permitted to evade.

Probably, the Earl appealed to the architectural aspirations of both Jones and the King by promoting a scheme which showed what might be done in a capital city. Certainly, it astonished Londoners.

THE PIAZZA

The most remarkable element in the building scheme was the Piazza, built between 1633 and 1637, a large open square now lost to view because its ground is covered by the former market building. On the west side was (and is) the classical church of St Paul's, the first Anglican church built in London since the mid-sixteenth century; on the north and east were residences that included an arcade beneath their upper storeys; on the south side was the wall of Bedford

House. The Piazza, a direct descendant of those seen by Jones in Italy – particularly that in Leghorn – was unadorned and open to the public, as indeed were the arcades inserted into the houses.

This was an infusion not just of classical architecture into London, but of a continental way of life in which the open square became a public meeting place and a location in which to sit and stare. Though the building of squares became common thereafter in London, they were always private squares, the designated territory of those whose houses surrounded them.

The Piazza's startling innovation is captured in early prints. The uniformity of the houses was remarkable in itself, and even the grid of uniform streets around was a new concept for most Londoners, who were used to their muddle of medieval streets, or else lanes following long-forgotten field boundaries.

Each of the seventeen porticoed residences in the Piazza had a mezzanine and ground floor (with basement underneath) fronting the rusticated arcade;

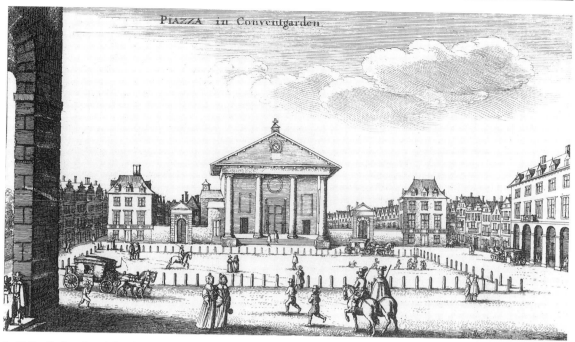

6. *St Paul's church and the Piazza, by Wenceslaus Hollar. The two houses on either side of the church were demolished in 1690 and 1730.*

above that were two brick storeys and a dormer divided by pilasters. Some idea of their style may be had from the present Bedford Chambers on the north side of the square, designed by Henry Clutton in the nineteenth century. Gradually, these uniform houses were taken down. Some on the south-east collapsed in 1670, were rebuilt and then rebuilt again in 1769 without arcades; the westernmost house of the north range (now No. 43 King Street) was demolished and replaced in 1717 by a Palladian house designed by Thomas Archer, which still stands. Four bays in the north-east corner were taken down in 1858 for the erection of the Floral Hall, and ten years later the rest of that range made way for the Tavistock Hotel. The last of them, on the north and east sides, were demolished c1933. There were also, as may be seen above, two smaller houses on either side of St Paul's church. One was rebuilt in 1690 in a different style and the other in 1730.

The fourth Earl had hoped for aristocratic tenants, or at least 'Persons of the greatest Distinction'. Certainly the early residents included many with titles, with at least three earls, but the Earl was unfortunate in timing. The Civil War, which began in 1642, brought unsettled conditions to the capital and, indeed, deterred many of the Earl's prospective tenants, if they had royalist sympathies, from living in London at all. It was not a time to sign leases and Covent Garden was unable to establish itself.

Nevertheless, the early tenants provided a hopeful start. They included Sir Henry Vane the younger at what is now 43 King Street, and another member of the Long Parliament, Sir Thomas Trenchard, at No. 1 Great Piazza; No. 3 had the Earl of Peterborough in 1639, and the president of the Royal Society, William Brouncker, was a later occupant in 1664. Sir William Alexander, first Earl of Stirling, poet and statesman, was at Nos 6-7 Great Piazza in 1638, to be followed by yet another Member of Parliament two years later. Denzil Holles, prominent member of the Long Parliament, was at Nos 16-17 in 1636.

But the Piazza's fame, at least as far as tenants go, rested on later, more artistic names. The dramatist, Thomas Killigrew, was first a tenant of No. 8 Great Piazza in 1636, but he returned in 1661-2 when he was building the first Theatre Royal, Drury Lane. The portrait painter, Sir Peter Lely, lived from 1651-80 at Nos 10-11, a house which was later taken by the famous actor, Charles Macklin. The painter, Sir James Thornhill, took No. 12 in 1722, and John Rich, manager of Covent Garden Theatre, was at No. 15 from 1743-60. Sir Godfrey Kneller, painter, lived at Nos 16-17 from 1682 to c1702.

The Civil War was not the only factor which prevented the Piazza and its surrounding streets from acquiring a firmly established aristocratic tenantry. Soon there were competitors – St James's Square, Bloomsbury Square, Soho Square, Golden Square.

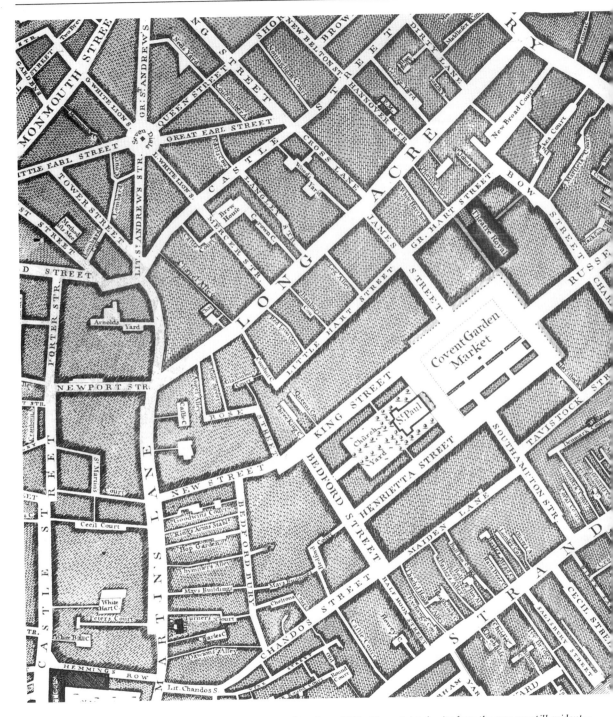

7. *The Covent Garden area as shown in John Rocque's map of London c.1746. The restricted exits from the area are still evident –
note the southern ends of Bedford Street and Drury Lane; Southampton Street was gated against market traffic and, as will be
seen, Garrick Street did not exist; access to Long Acre was through a narrow part of James Street.*

Drury Lane sweeps round to the east into Wych Street which came out by St Clement Danes church. The tightly packed courtyards of this area became notorious in the eighteenth century for gin shops and brothels. Burleigh Street is still a dead end, and has not yet been cut through to Tavistock Street. To the north-east of the Piazza is the 'Theatre Royal'. This is, in fact, the Covent Garden Theatre.

8. Sir Peter Lely, resident in the Piazza, from a self-portrait.

9. Sir Godfrey Kneller.

10. The actor, Charles Macklin, who made an appearance at Covent Garden Theatre as Shylock at the age of 89.

All these offered seclusion to those who could afford it. No strangers in these squares sheltered from the rain in an arcade just outside your front room; no-one managed a fruit stall in full view of your ground-floor window, or cleaned shoes; no-one, indeed, ventured onto the pavement around the square unless he or she had legitimate business. And there were certainly no stalls selling fruit and vegetables in the square itself – a practice increasingly common in Covent Garden.

The south side of the Piazza was not begun until the demolition of Bedford House in 1706, when the second Duke of Bedford moved to a new mansion he had erected on the north side of his own Bloomsbury Square – the ground landlord of Covent Garden himself thus contributing towards a liking for the privacy of the newer London squares. By 1714 fourteen houses without arcades, called Tavistock Row, had been built on the land now taken by the Jubilee Hall and adjacent buildings.

11. Houses on the Little Piazza. This group of houses was on the south-east side of the square; their site today is taken by Russell Chambers and the London Transport Museum. The house on the right contains the Old Hummums, a Turkish bath which occasionally had a reputation for being rather more than that.

THE INNER STREETS

By April 1631 the principal streets of Covent Garden were planned and given names that commemorated either the royal family or the Bedford family. The main streets took the more obsequious names – King, James and Henrietta – and there was also a Charles Street which became the top end of Wellington Street, and a York Street, now the eastern end of Tavistock Street. The Bedford family were represented in, of course, Bedford and Russell Streets, and also in Brydges Street, now part of Catherine Street, and Tavistock Street. Maiden Lane, probably a remnant of an ancient trackway from St Martin's Lane to Drury Lane behind the houses of the Strand, is first encountered as a name in 1636; it may be much older and its name merely, as in other localities, a corruption of 'midden', meaning rubbish or dungheap.

Oddly, the Earl did not or could not make access to his scheme of spacious streets convenient for either residents or visitors. Particularly, it was difficult to get into the Strand. Southampton Street did not then exist, since Bedford House stood on its site, and the full width of Bedford Street ended as it does today at the junction with Maiden Lane, terminating in what was then just an alley to the Strand. Russell Street and Tavistock Street connected with Bow Street, but there was no southern exit from Bow Street and travellers had to find their way into Drury Lane which itself connected to the Strand by a very narrow outlet. The construction of Catherine Street in 1673 improved matters but it was not until 1835 that Wellington Street was completed, so that it was possible to travel down Bow Street to Waterloo Bridge. To the west, Garrick Street did not exist and access to Covent Garden was via the narrow New Row. The outlet of James Street into Long Acre was also extremely restricted. It is no wonder that residents in 1638 complained about the 'narrow and crooked passages that leade unto the high streetes'. Things were made worse when the market grew to cover the open piazza and the Bedford Estate placed barriers to prevent market traffic spilling into King and Henrietta Streets.

As its name implies, King Street was the grander of the streets, and the houses on its north side were of greater quality than those on its south which backed on to the churchyard. Those on the north had yards, stables and coachhouses extending into Hart Street, subsequently renamed Floral Street. None of the original buildings of 1633-7 in this street survives.

Though seven titled people are listed as living in King Street in 1672, a good many 'eminent' tradesmen, as London historian John Strype called them, also occupied houses here from the 1670s. At No. 31,

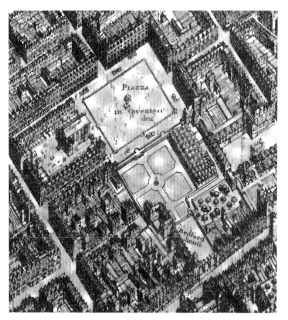

12. *Section of a bird's-eye map of London by Wenceslaus Hollar, mid-seventeenth century. It shows Bedford House on the north side of the Strand, with its gardens backing on to the Piazza.*

for example, a house rebuilt in 1713, the first occupant was an upholsterer, Thomas Arne, whose son, the future composer of *Rule Britannia*, spent part of his boyhood here – he had, in fact, been born in the house that previously existed on the site, which had been destroyed by fire.

The oldest surviving house in this street is No. 43, on the site of the most western of the arcaded houses of the Piazza. The original house had been that of Admiral Edward Russell (1653-1727), grandson of the 4th Earl of Bedford, who later played a prominent part in the establishment of William of Orange on the English throne. He was created Earl of Orford in 1697 and in 1716, as a condition of a new lease, was required to build a new house on the site. This new building, apparently designed by Thomas Archer to whom Orford was related, was completed in 1717. The old arcade was excluded though the building line was perpetuated and there is to this day a door, albeit now unusable, from the side of Orford's house into the nineteenth-century arcade beneath Bedford Chambers. Archer eventually acquired the house himself – a rare example of an architect living in a house he had designed. We may regard Thomas Archer House with some pleasure now, but the architect, Batty

13. *No. 43 King Street, built c1717 and designed by Thomas Archer. It replaced one of the arcaded houses, shown to the right of the picture.*

14. *The arcades beneath the Piazza houses, in the north-eastern corner of the square.*

Langley, writing in 1734, remarked that it 'is certainly one of the most expensive and worst buildings about London....' There is little left in the house from that period. Two rooms on the first floor are fairly well preserved, but its subsequent history as a hotel and the offices of a market trader did not treat it kindly.

Despite King Street's general decline from the Bedford expectations, it remained a good address and did not succumb to market trading until the turn of this century.

The narrow Floral Street, on the other hand, with its south side partly occupied by the rear yards of King Street, went downhill very quickly in social clout. Some middle-class tenants are recorded in its early days, but by mid-seventeenth century there were tailors and barbers here and by the end of that century nine licensed victuallers. The street's status was confirmed in 1703 when the parish authorities took a house here to contain the poor, and by the early nineteenth century Floral Street was known for its disorderly houses.

A similar linking of streets occurred between Henrietta Street and Maiden Lane, where the premises of the former stretched into the latter. Again, nothing of the earliest buildings remains in Henrietta Street and most of the premises were rebuilt for at least the second time in the nineteenth century. From the

beginning it was a 'trade' street – two shoemakers and four licensed victuallers were among its first occupants. In 1720 Strype described the houses as 'generally being taken up by eminent Tradesmen, as Mercers, Lacemen, Drapers, etc'. Samuel Scott, the artist, lived at No. 2 from 1747 to 1758. Between 1806 and 1816, No. 10 was occupied by the bank of Austen, Maunde and Tilson. The Austen was Jane Austen's brother and she stayed here twice on trips to London.

The earliest residents of Bedford Street included some with titles, and in 1635 Sir Francis Kynaston's Musæum Minervæ, an academy for young gentlemen and noblemen who were educated in 'armes and artes and all generous qualities', was established in a house opposite the churchyard gates. It was an adventurous and comprehensive enterprise to which Charles I gave encouragement and endorsement, but it survived only two to three years. The subjects on offer ranged from fencing to astronomy, optics to heraldry, music to mathematics; one professor taught seven languages.

Russell Street is the broadest street of the scheme, as wide as the portico of the St Paul's church it faced across the Piazza. But despite this generous width it did not attract the tenants desired by the 4th Earl and its character was changed anyway by the opening of the Theatre Royal in 1674 and Covent Garden Theatre in 1732, which drew the street into their ambience and nightlife. It became the liveliest of streets, full of tradesmen, coffee houses, taverns and lodging houses – John Evelyn stayed there in 1659-60 as did Charles Lamb and his sister in 1820.

At No. 8 Russell Street was Davies's bookshop, in which James Boswell first met Dr Johnson in 1763. Boswell describes the event:

'Mr Davies, the actor, who then kept a bookseller's shop in Russell Street, Covent Garden, told me that Johnson was very much his friend, and came frequently to his house, where he more than once invited me to meet him; but by some unlucky accident or other he was prevented from coming to us.

At last, on Monday the 16th of May when I was sitting in Mr Davies's back parlour, after having drunk tea with him and Mrs Davies, Johnson unexpectedly came into the shop; and Mr Davies having perceived him, through the glass-door in the room in which we were sitting, advancing towards us, he announced his awful approach to me, somewhat in the manner of an actor in the part of Horatio, when he addresses Hamlet on the appearance of his father's ghost, "Look, my lord, it comes!"'

Davies, knowing Johnson's aversion to Scotsmen, mischievously told Johnson that Boswell was Scots and Boswell in some embarrassment said "I do indeed come from Scotland, but I cannot help it." "That Sir," replied Johnson, "I find is what a very great many of your countrymen cannot help."

Russell Street had its seedier nature. The original William Hickey (1749-1830) recalled going to one of the more disreputable houses there with friends one evening. They were scrutinised at the door by a 'cutthroat looking rascal' peering through a small wicket before admission. The first titillation offered them was that of two half-naked, bleeding and wholly drunken women having a wrestling match. Later, 'an uncommonly athletic young man of about twenty-five' was introduced whose role was to be attacked by 'no less than three Amazonian tigresses with sticks.'

Southampton Street was laid out as from the end of 1706 across the site and gardens of Bedford House. The Bedford Estate jealously guarded this new street from the market and through traffic in general. As early as 1739 it reminded an occupant that 'this street in particular, by the Vigilant & prudent care of his Grace's Ancestors, has been constantly kept free from the passage of heavy and burdensome Carriages which are permitted upon sufferance only, & that upon extraordinary occasions.' To this end a gate with a gatehouse was erected at the lower end of the road to stop vehicles entering from the Strand. The street's architectural appearance may be judged by the two surviving houses, Nos. 26 and 27, though the fronts have been altered somewhat. No. 27 was the home of the actor, David Garrick, from 1749 until 1772 and was, in more recent years, the office of the theat-

15. Hustings for Parliamentary elections were often held in the Piazza. This illustration, by Pugin and Rowlandson, depicting the Westminster election, was published between 1808-10.

16. *Tom Davies' bookshop at 8 Russell Street; drawing by Hanslip Fletcher.*

17. *Dr Samuel Johnson, by Joshua Reynolds, 1770.*

rical publishers, Samuel French.

James Street was of sufficient stature when built to contain the parsonage (at No. 27) of St Paul's church, but the use of the street by market traders ensured its decline in comparison with the estate's better streets. Garrick lodged here before he set up home in Southampton Street.

Catherine Street was built in two parts. The upper section, north of Exeter Street, was laid out in the 1630s and called Brydges Street after the family name of the 4th Earl of Bedford's wife. The way out to the Strand was originally blocked by the White Hart Inn and the grounds of Exeter House in the Strand, but in 1657 an alleyway was formed to the Strand; when, in 1673, the inn was demolished Catherine Street was built to the Strand, named in honour of Charles II's queen.

Tavistock Street was built in three parts, the first between what are now Wellington Street and Catherine Street in the 1630s, and named then as York Street. After Bedford House was demolished in 1706 the next section was constructed between Southampton Street and York Street. Finally, in 1900 an extension was made east to Drury Lane and across the old St Mary-le-Strand burial ground. The three sections were renamed as Tavistock Street in 1937.

18. *James Boswell.*

19. *St Paul's church, east front, in 1968.*

The Church in the Piazza

The building of St Paul's church, which began in 1631, was as much an innovation as the Piazza itself. It was not only the first new Anglican church to be built in London for nearly a century (St Katharine Cree in the City was rebuilt 1628-30), it was the first classical church in the capital. It was erected at a time when controversy as to the nature of church buildings was at its height, and this simple and delightful Tuscan structure was the object of much suspicion and criticism.

Designed by Inigo Jones, St Paul's was a carefully costed building. The 4th Earl of Bedford had little choice but to provide a church in his new development, since its presence would influence the sale of building leases in the surrounding streets. There is evidence that the Earl wanted nothing elaborate, but then again he would not have wanted a building that either marred or undermined the quality of his development. There is a famous anecdote, retold by Horace Walpole, of a conversation between the Earl and

Jones, that may or may not be true, which has the Earl instructing the architect that 'he wou'd not go to any considerable expense; in short, said he, I wou'd not have it much better than a barn. Well! then, replied Jones, you shall have the handsomest barn in England.'

More significant than the Earl's notorious thrift, were the religious disputes of the time. Jones himself owed his livelihood to the patronage of the Crown, but the Earl was a confirmed reformist and Puritan in church matters, at odds with the views of Laud, Charles I's Bishop of London. Stemming from the arguments of the day is the odd feature that the east door of the church, one that should open on to the Piazza, is a false one, for behind it lies the altar. Architecturally this was the most appropriate place to have the main entrance and so it was planned, but the Laudian administration insisted while the church was being built that the door should be moved to the west end of the building, where it now is, and the altar placed, as was traditionally the case, at the east.

This reorientation was, as it turned out, beneficial, for the entrance from the churchyard was better placed once the market had grown in both size and

20. *The main entrance and churchyard of St Paul's Covent Garden. From a watercolour in the Sir John Soane Museum.*

noise, and in modern times the unused east portico has provided a backdrop for numerous entertainments. But it could not have pleased Jones to have had his masterpiece tampered with.

Not everyone has liked the church. Horace Walpole was distinctly lukewarm, asking 'Whoever saw a beautiful Tuscan building? Would the Romans have chose that order for a temple?' A large number of parishioners of St Martin-in-the-Fields, on whom the expense of its maintenance was to devolve, complained to the king that it was a chapel, not a church. It was they who would have to bear the expense of erecting a steeple above it, they complained.

The building is 100ft x 50ft and its severely simple interior is without division in the body of the church, and between nave and chancel. It did not at first have galleries, but these were inserted later to house the increasing population of the area. The most prominent features of the exterior are the large pediments at both ends of the church, and the unusually wide eaves that extend well beyond the walls of the building.

St Paul's remained unconsecrated until 1638 due to contention over the patronage of the living between the Earl and the vicar of St Martin-in-the-Fields, and its parochial status was left unresolved because of the Civil War. At the Restoration the parish of St Paul's was carved out of the territory of St Martin's.

In 1788 work began on a major restoration of the building, supervised by the architect, Thomas Hardwick. The stucco on the exterior walls favoured

21. *Dr. Thomas Arne.*

22. *Grinling Gibbons, from a portrait by Sir Godfrey Kneller.*

is now Inigo Place off Bedford Street. Previously, this ground, like all other London burial grounds, had been overcrowded, especially with paupers' graves, and it is likely that the vault constructed beneath the church in 1756 was also full as well.

St Paul's has become known as the 'Actors' Church' and it is here that many memorial services are held for members of the theatrical profession. This is in part due to the number that had already been buried here in previous centuries – William Wycherley and Charles Macklin for example – but the church is adjacent to what used to be the centre of London's theatreland around Drury Lane and the Strand. Others interred here were Grinling Gibbons, the wood carver and artist, painter Sir Peter Lely, the satirist Samuel But-ler, the artist Thomas Rowlandson, and the composer Thomas Arne. It is also thought that Claud Duval, the celebrated highwayman, was buried here after his execution. The ashes of Ellen Terry are kept in a casket on the south wall, but otherwise today the extent of remembrance will be a plaque on the walls such as those for Noel Coward, Bransby Williams, Ivor Novello and Charles B. Cochrane. The artist J.M.W. Turner, was baptised here in 1775 – his par-ents, who were married in the church, lived in Maiden Lane.

by Jones was replaced by Portland stone which was better wearing, the old ceiling taken down and vari-ous other changes made, though there were still structural problems after this. But misfortune was to follow. In September 1795 builders working in the bell turret left a fire unattended and caused the de-struction of the church with the exception of the walls, portico and south-west wing. It was an expensive fire because the parish had failed to renew its insurance policy and had to find the cost of rebuilding out of parish rates. The work was entrusted to Hardwick whose knowledge of the church was still fresh and he created a building which, in most respects, faithfully replicated the design of Inigo Jones.

The churchyard today is one of the marvellous, rather secretive gardens that abound in London. It is entered by two small gates from King Street and Henrietta Street, and through a main gate from what

23. *Interior of St Paul's church in 1968.*

The Beginnings of a Market

It seems puzzling in retrospect that the 4th Earl of Bedford, intent on attracting people of distinction to his new development, should also permit a small market in the Piazza from quite early times. Robert Thorne, in his excellent account of the market's history (see bibliography), notes that the first mention of traders here is as early as 1649. Then the City Corporation protested at a breach of its monopoly over markets within seven miles of the City walls, although a painting of the Piazza of the same year does not depict any traders in the square. But, in 1654, one Thomas Cotton is described as living 'about the new market in Covent Garden' and a view of 1666 has traders assembled to the south of the square.

One answer to the puzzle may simply be that there were not at a convenient distance any other market facilities for the residents of Covent Garden nor fresh food places nearby. How the Earl was able to contravene the City's monopoly with impunity is unclear, but the problems of affirming and enforcing monopoly privileges during the Civil War may have led to a relaxation which, by the time of the Restoration, was difficult to reverse. It may be that at first the Earl derived no toll income from the market and was therefore not technically in breach of the City's monopoly. The situation was, however, changed completely in 1666 when the Great Fire of London rendered the City virtually uninhabitable and its traditional markets were destroyed. Suffice to say that in 1670 the market at Covent Garden was so well established that the Earl was able to obtain an official charter to manage it and to charge tolls, though the terms were unspecific in respect of these.

The charter was more detailed in the matter of the area the market might cover, for it permitted the use of the whole of the Piazza, an extraordinary freedom at a time when the market was probably quite small and confined to part of the south side. Even as late as 1741 the stalls and sheds extended little further north than that so that it was still possible to have an uninterrupted view of the portico of St Paul's from Russell Street, and it was probably contrived that way in any case. But by the 1760s the market occupied much of the Piazza, inside a railed area, though actual market buildings were still kept to the south so as to preserve the portico vista.

From these small beginnings rose the largest fruit and vegetable market in the country and, with one small exception, the only privately owned market in the London area, an exclusiveness which, as time went on, was regarded with increasing hostility. The looseness of the original charter of 1670 often made the assessment of tolls a matter for negotiation, since it was impossible to arrive at an exact figure which reference to the charter could support. There are thus innumerable cases of traders protesting against the tolls and as late as 1817 even the right to levy them was challenged in the courts.

24. A view of Covent Garden market, published in 1746. By this time trading (but not buildings) had extended to the northern side of the square.

25. *Covent Garden market at the turn of the nineteenth century. Miscellaneous sheds were now a feature of the northern part of the square.*

At the Restoration the church side of the Piazza was also being used for entertainments. Pepys went to a puppet show with his wife in 1662 and in 1711 a correspondent to the *Spectator* complains that members of St Paul's congregation now prefer to see the puppet shows than go to services.

As the market expanded in size during the nineteenth century the Bedford family, sitting on a lucrative source of income and now without the incentive to keep up the residential status of the area, was able to house the market in new buildings both in and outside the Piazza. In providing them, as is pointed out in the *Survey of London* volume dealing with Covent Garden, the Bedfords knocked down houses in nearby residential streets and, in effect, extended the market beyond the Piazza, whatever the charter had to say. In this situation, where the Bedfords owned the streets, they were able to encourage developments and respond to them.

The original charter authorised the sale of fruit, flowers, roots and herbs, but it is apparent that other goods were soon to be found there, including cage birds. In 1748 local residents complained that for some years past many of the stalls had been occupied by 'Bakers, Haberdashers, Cook shops, Retailers of Geneva and Other Spirituous Liquors'. Others had converted the permanent shop lofts into small bedrooms so that the 'stench and filth of the Markett, the Offensive Smoke of the chimneys of the said several Sheds and the Disturbances which frequently happen, by the great Number of profligate and disorderly people, who frequent the Square, and particularly that part of it called Irish Row'.

Order was restored, though the problem of prostitutes patrolling the square could never be remedied. The traders sorted themselves out, just as they had done on the floor of Gresham's Royal Exchange in the City, so that it was possible for retailers more easily to find specialists. Florists were on the west side, herbs and potatoes on the south, vegetables on the north and various fruits and beans on the east. But some other specialties survived, such as crockery sellers in the centre. James Street on Sunday mornings contained a bird market at which it was possible to buy magpies, sparrows and linnets.

Enter the Stage

THE CREATION OF A MONOPOLY

Before the Civil War of the seventeenth century theatre flourished, with some limitations, in Southwark. In theory and to an extent in practice Southwark was under the control of the City, which had a partial remit to govern, but there is no doubt that the south bank's attractions, artistic, brutal and venal, were realistically tolerated. However, the Puritans had no truck with such *laissez-faire* policies and theatre largely disappeared from London during the Commonwealth.

An exception, though of little artistic value, was the Cockpit, off Drury Lane. This was built in 1609, as its name suggests, originally as a cockpit, but in 1616 it was converted to a theatre. The following year the self-appointed and boisterous guardians of London morals, the London apprentices, used their traditional rioting day of Shrove Tuesday to wreck the building. But it recovered, and was still in business until Parliamentary troops demolished it in 1649. Aptly called the Phoenix, it rose again, and was still used for drama and opera during the Commonwealth, as we know from the journals of John Evelyn.

Despite its necessarily inglorious existence during a period when anything decorative was officially abhorred, the Cockpit was the seed which eventually sprouted as the Theatre Royal, Drury Lane.

At the Restoration in 1660 theatre was still regarded with some suspicion by the authorities. It could, after all, be a medium for political opposition, and it therefore needed control. The Restoration did not restore freedom of political discussion, as the publishers of newspapers and broadsheets were to discover, and theatre, though revived, was still seriously curtailed. In 1660 the Crown granted two patents, ratified in 1663, for the erection of two playhouses in London or Westminster and the creation of two companies of players. No other licences were issued permitting the production of plays and this monopoly held, at least in theory, until 1843. The recipients of this royal favour, both dramatists themselves, were Thomas Killigrew and Sir William Davenant.

Killigrew had long been familiar with Court, first as a page to Charles I, for whom he took up arms in 1642. He was then an emissary to Venice for the exiled Charles II, for whom he gathered funds, but he was expelled from this post for debauchery. Despite this, he was regarded as part of the household of Charles II after the Restoration, and it was his theatrical company which was called 'The King's Servants'.

27. Sir William Davenant.

26. Thomas Killigrew.

Davenant had been appointed 'governor of the King and Queen's Company', acting at the Cockpit in 1639, in a period when it was necessary for theatrical companies to seek the protection of key figures at Court to avoid harassment by religious bigots. But Davenant's theatrical career was interrupted by the growing hostility between Parliament and the King and he was implicated in a scheme to secure aid for Charles I in 1641. He took flight to France but returned to England on several occasions to help in the unsuccessful royalist cause; in 1650 he began a two-year sentence in the Tower of London for doing so. Such was the unpredictability of the age that by 1657 he was to be found in London producing musical plays at the Cockpit with the permission of the Commonwealth government – anodyne presentations that sustained him but avoided prosecution. However, upon the Restoration he set up his own theatre company under the protection of the King's brother, the Duke of York, the future James II (Davenant had already converted to Catholicism).

Granting only two licences to produce plays therefore restricted the number of theatres which could be sustained in London. Drama was staged at the rather makeshift Salisbury Court theatre, off Fleet Street, soon after the Restoration, in which Davenant some-

times took part. In 1661, armed with his patent, he opened a new theatre near Lincoln's Inn Fields on the site of some tennis courts, which was the first in London to have a proscenium arch (Davenant was also the first to use movable scenery). Much of the Fleet Street area was destroyed in the Great Fire, including the Salisbury Court theatre, and at the time of his death in 1668 Davenant was engaged in the construction of a magnificent building designed by Wren, the Dorset Gardens Theatre, between Fleet Street and the Thames, which opened in 1671.

THE THEATRE ROYAL

Meanwhile, Killigrew had obtained from the Earl of Bedford a lease of land in Riding Yard, between Drury Lane and today's Catherine Street, to erect a playhouse. This small building, measuring just 112ft x 59ft, opened in 1663 with a performance of Beaumont and Fletcher's *The Humorous Lieutenant* and in 1664 he staged *The Parson's Wedding*, a play that was acted only by women on account of its obscenity. Samuel Pepys was a frequent visitor and noted after its second day's performance that 'The house is made with

29. John Rich as Harlequin, 1753.

28. Nell Gwyn, from a painting by Sir Peter Lely.

30. *The interior of the first Covent Garden Theatre; aquatint by Thomas Rowlandson.*

extraordinary good convenience and yet hath some faults, as the narrowness of the passage in and out of the Pit, and the distance from the Stage to the Boxes.' It was in this building in 1665 that Nell Gwyn made her stage debut in a play by Dryden.

No illustration of this first Theatre Royal has been discovered. It was burned down in 1672 (together with about fifty houses in the vicinity) and Killigrew moved out temporarily to the Lincoln's Inn theatre which had recently been vacated by Davenant's company.

Christopher Wren designed the succeeding Theatre Royal in 1674, described by Dryden as 'plain built – a bare convenience only'. Its foundations may still be seen beneath the present stage. This period was marked by disputes between the two licensed acting companies, but in November 1682 they merged to perform at the Theatre Royal, which meant that only one theatre could present plays in London. After Killigrew's death the following year both patents came into the hands of Christopher Rich. He was never a popular owner and disagreements continued for several years. Some idea of their nature may be gained from an account by the actor, Colley Cibber. 'One only theatre being now in the possession of the whole town the united patentees imposed their terms upon the actors; for the profits of acting were then divided into twenty shares, ten of which went to the proprietors, and the other moiety to the principal actors, in such subdivisions as their different merits might pretend to do.... which occasioned great contention between the patentees and performers.' In 1711 Rich was edged out of the Theatre Royal, leaving Cibber in charge and in possession of Killigrew's patent.

COVENT GARDEN THEATRE

Christopher Rich moved to the old Lincoln's Inn theatre, which he planned to rebuild, but he died before it reopened in 1714. His son, John Rich, succeeded him and was responsible for the debut at Lincoln's Inn of John Gay's *The Beggar's Opera* which, wags noted at the time, was successful enough to make 'Gay rich and Rich gay'. Still holding Davenant's old patent, John Rich built a new theatre in Bow Street, Covent Garden in 1732, designed by Edward Shepherd: its descendant is the present Royal Opera House. The first production was Congreve's *The Way of the World*. Thus, from this date and until an Act of 1843 tided matters up, the only two theatres in London permitted to stage plays were in Covent Garden. Any other promoter had to ensure that his play was essentially musical to escape this monopoly.

Ironically, by the time Covent Garden Theatre was built, opera and pantomime were the rage and not drama. Opera had been so popular at what is now Her Majesty's Theatre in the Haymarket, built originally by Vanbrugh in 1703, that Covent Garden was obliged to alternate between drama and opera. Her Majesty's Theatre had been poor competition at first, precluded as it was from staging drama. And, as Cibber noted at the time, the theatre audience was deterred from going so far west: 'The City, Inns of Court and the middle part of town, which were the most constant support of a theatre.... were too far out of the reach of an easy walk and coach hire is often too hard a tax upon the Pit and the Gallery.' But in the 1720s, when Her Majesty's introduced Handel opera and then Italian opera, the theatre-going population of London had moved westwards slightly and found the location of the Haymarket quite convenient.

31. *The third Theatre Royal, Drury Lane, designed by Henry Holland and opened in 1794.*

SUCCESS AT THE THEATRE ROYAL

Drama had a difficult time at the Theatre Royal in Drury Lane as well. There had also been an unfortunate evening when the management introduced a rule precluding the free entry of the footmen who attended the gentlemen in the audience. This so enraged the servants that they stormed the theatre and tried to set fire to it. Fortunes changed in 1742 when the young David Garrick was persuaded to transfer from the theatre in Goodman's Fields in the East End, where he had been a sensational Richard III in a production punctuated by musical interludes to conform to the patent regulations. He was equally successful at Drury Lane. Here he played Hamlet to the Ophelia of Peg Woffington, an actress who had taken Covent Garden Theatre by storm when she first appeared there in 1740. Garrick's arrival at the Theatre Royal was the beginning of a successful era and five years later he was joint owner of the patent, having paid £8,000 for it.

Garrick did not retire from the management of the Theatre Royal until 1776, the year after Sarah Siddons had made her (unsuccessful) debut there. The theatre was then taken over by Richard Brinsley Sheridan, whose *School for Scandal* was first produced there in 1770; the actor, John Philip Kemble, took over the management in 1788. By that time Wren's building was in a poor state and three years later rebuilding began.

The new theatre, opened in 1794, was by the architect Henry Holland. It was a short-lived venture, for in February 1809, not yet paid for and underinsured, it was destroyed by fire. Sheridan, who still held the patent and who had a good deal of money invested in it, watched the building blaze from a nearby house and calmly remarked that 'surely a gentleman may warm his hands at his own fireside.'

The present theatre, designed by Benjamin Wyatt, was opened in 1812. One of its financial backers was Samuel Whitbread, brewer and politician, whose investment made good the losses of Sheridan. However, the new theatre plunged into difficulties and even in 1814, when Edmund Kean made a spectacular debut, the theatre lost £20,000 and Whitbread committed suicide.

32. The fire which destroyed the third Theatre Royal Drury Lane in 1809, viewed from south of the river.

The Ruins of the Theatre from Bridges Street, after the Fire.

33. *(Above) The ruins of the third Theatre Royal, Drury Lane, after the fire in 1809.*

34. *(Below) The fourth, and present, Theatre Royal, Drury Lane, erected in 1812. The portico and colonnade seen today were erected later.*

35. *(Right) Richard Brinsley Sheridan.*

OPERA IN BOW STREET

Covent Garden Theatre too had been contributing to theatre history in the meantime. In 1773 Goldsmith's *She Stoops to Conquer* was first seen there – the playwright so nervous as to its success that he brought in friends to applaud and did not dare watch until the final act. Two years later came the first showing of Sheridan's *The Rivals*. The child prodigy, William Betty, began his London career here as a tragedian in 1804.

However, disaster struck in 1808 when, as with the Drury Lane theatre the following year, it was destroyed by fire, with the loss of the organ used by Handel and many of his manuscripts. The new theatre, opened in 1809, was modelled by Robert Smirke on the Temple of Minerva at Athens. The cost of its construction obliged the management to increase ticket prices above those charged for the previous building and this provoked organised demonstrations outside for sixty-six nights, so that the Riot Act had to be read. But public demand won and the old prices were reinstated.

First performances included Mozart's *Don Giovanni* (1817), *The Marriage of Figaro* (1819) and Rossini's *Barber of Seville* (1818). Sarah Siddons made her last London performance here in 1812 and William Macready, the new London star, made his debut in

37. *William Macready, the new star on the London scene, made his debut at Covent Garden Theatre.*

36. *The second Covent Garden Theatre, designed by Sir Robert Smirke.*

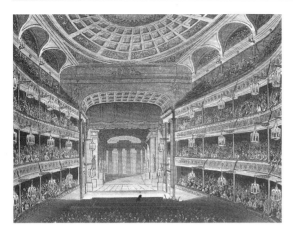

38. *Interior of the second Covent Garden Theatre, depicted by Pugin and Rowlandson, c1809.*

39. *Sarah Siddons, who made her last London performance at Covent Garden in 1812. Oil sketch by George Romney.*

40. *The Strand front of the old Lyceum. The words 'Theatre Royal' emblazoned on the upper part of the building, indicate that this illustration was made after the fire at the Theatre Royal, Drury Lane in 1809, which obliged the acting company to remove temporarily to the Lyceum. Drury Lane was reopened in 1812.*

41. *Interior of the first Lyceum in 1790; drawing by J. Winston.*

1816. Gaslight was introduced in parts of Covent Garden Theatre in 1815-16 – soon to be adopted at Drury Lane.

Once again fire intruded in Bow Street. Smirke's building was burned down in 1856 and the present building, designed by E.M. Barry (who also built the glass and iron Floral Hall next door) was erected in about eight months to the accompaniment of wagers as to its likely completion date.

THE LYCEUM

By this time a potential rival had been built around the corner in Wellington Street – the Lyceum, a theatre to have its own history of fires. The original Lyceum was built in 1772 at the eastern end of the Strand as a venue for art exhibitions, concerts and minor entertainments, but by 1799 it was also presenting a mixture of drama and music adeptly fashioned to keep within the law. Madame Tussaud presented her first London waxworks here in 1802. The Lyceum became a legitimate theatre in 1809 after the destruction by fire of the Theatre Royal, when the Drury Lane company transferred here and the management was able to hold on to the licence for staging plays in the summer months once the new theatre in Drury Lane had been opened. The Lyceum was rebuilt in 1816 in classical style by Samuel Beazley, but was burned down in 1830.

Beazley was again the architect when a new Lyceum was built (in four months) in 1834 at the southern end of Wellington Street, then a newly-constructed thoroughfare linking Bow Street with Waterloo Bridge. Little except the portico remains of that building, which had its first heyday in the 1840s during the management of Charles Mathews and his wife, Madame Vestris. Its main contribution to English theatre was made after 1878 during the management of Henry Irving, who employed Ellen Terry as his leading lady. In 1904 the Lyceum was reconstructed as a music hall.

42. *Rooftop view of the original Lyceum, 1790. Drawing by J. Winston.*

43. *The new Lyceum building, designed by Samuel Beazley. The portico still stands outside the present building.*

Seven Dials

Seven Dials, now an area of niche shops, boutiques and restaurants, was one of the great slums of London, rivalling the nearby St Giles's Rookery for infamy. The building scheme for the area, instigated by Sir Thomas Neale in the 1690s, was a speculative failure and the quality of buildings was insufficient to prevent it from deteriorating. When rebuilding came the area's reputation was such that new premises were of a poor quality. Its nearness to Covent Garden market, where occasional labour might be had, led to it being let as overcrowded lodging houses for itinerant workers, with the concomitant trades of second-hand clothes and gin shops inevitably present.

44. 'Plan of proposed setting out of Seven Dials 1691'. The plan is rather misleading since Monmouth Street, which is the present-day main axis of the scheme, was the name of a road to the west, which is now the line of Shaftesbury Avenue. St Andrew Street is today's Monmouth Street, Earl Street is now Earlham Street, Queen Street is Shorts Gardens and Little Monmouth Street is the western end of Mercer Street. The eastern end of Mercer Street was added after this plan. Castle Street is today called Shelton Street.

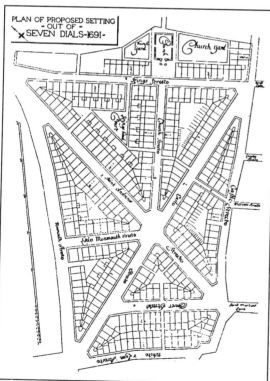

It began more grandly. John Evelyn reported in 1694 that he had been to see 'the building beginning neere St Giles's where 7 streetes make a star from a Doric pillar plac'd in the middle of a circular area; said to be by Mr Neale, introducer of the late Lotteries in imitation of those at Venice.'

Neale (*d.*1699?), for whom Neal Street is named, seems to have been a man of parts. He was both Master of the Royal Mint and groom-porter to Charles II and William III, the latter sinecure involving the furnishing of the king's lodgings, the provision of cards and dice, and the settling of any disputes which arose at the card table or on the bowling green. In 1684 in this capacity he was also empowered to license and suppress gaming houses and, given the corruption of the times, he probably enriched himself in the process. He appears, as Evelyn suggests, to have masterminded the lottery introduced in 1694, which was

45. The six-dial pillar, re-erected in Weybridge, c1914.

based on the security of a new Salt Tax, and which not only gave prizes but provided income from investment. In 1695 his name appears as one of the promoters of the National Land Bank, a device to establish a fund which could be drawn upon by the Crown, just as the Bank of England had been formed a year earlier with a similar facility. He also embarked on another development in London, when he obtained from Sir Thomas Clarges the lease on a large slice of land to the north of Piccadilly, but being short of money he let the land lay waste and died insolvent with no buildings erected.

Oddly, the pillar from which Seven Dials derives its name had six sundials and not seven. An early plan of Neale's development, drawn up in 1691 before building commenced, proposed only six streets radiating from the pillar and presumably a change of plan occurred after the pillar had been fashioned. What is now the east end of Mercer Street was the later addition to the scheme. The old pillar still survives. It was taken down in 1773 on the (erroneous) supposition that a large sum of money was to be found beneath it and moved to Sayes Court, Addlestone where it lay neglected for many years until the inhabitants of Weybridge bought it and erected it as a

47. *'Gin Lane' by William Hogarth. Familiar with this part of London, the artist probably had in mind the rookeries at St Giles and Seven Dials.*

46. *Dudley Street, Seven Dials, as depicted by Doré, published in 1872.*

48. A depressingly dirty Neal Street at the end of the nineteenth century.

tribute to a local resident, Frederica, Duchess of York. The dials were removed and a coronet placed on the top instead.

John Gay, writing in 1716 in *Trivia*, mentions narrow alleys and winding courts, and the area was renowned for its ballad printers and singers, the best known of which was James Catnach, whose premises were in one of the courtyards.

Dickens, who had a sharp eye for the sleazier parts of London, describes Seven Dials in *Sketches by Boz*:

The stranger who finds himself in the Dials for the first time... at the entrance of seven obscure passages, uncertain which to take, will see enough around him to keep his curiosity and attention awake for no inconsiderable time. From the irregular square into which he has plunged, the streets and courts dart in all directions, until they are lost in the unwholesome vapour which hangs over the house-tops, and renders the dirty perspective uncertain and confined; and lounging at every corner, as if they came there to take a few gasps of such fresh air as has found its way so far, but is too much exhausted already to be enabled to force itself into the narrow alleys around, are groups of people, whose appearance and dwellings would fill any mind but a regular Londoner's with astonishment.... In addition to the numerous groups who are idling about the ginshops, and squabbling in the centre of the road, every post in the open space has its occupant who leans against it for hours with listless perseverance.

Writing nine years after his father's death, Charles Dickens jnr in 1879 describes the kind of shops in the area.

.... the stranger finds himself in a street altogether unique in its way. It is the abode of bird-fanciers. Every variety of pigeon, fowl and rabbit can be found here, together with rare birds, such as hawks and owls, parrots, love-birds, and other species native and foreign. There is a shop for specimens for aquaria, with its tanks of water-beetles, newts, water-spiders and other aquatic creatures.'

Referring to the poverty of Seven Dials, Dickens jnr goes on:

Here poverty is to be seen in its most painful features. The shops sell nothing but second or third hand articles – old dresses, old clothes, old hats, and at the top of the stairs of little underground cellars, old shoes, so patched and

49.   *The junction of Earlham Street and Shelton Street, probably early in the nineteenth century. The smoke from the buildings on the left is probably from the large Combe & Delafield brewery.*

mended that it is questionable whether one particle of the original material remains in them. These streets swarm with children of all ages, engaged in any kind of game which childhood is capable of enjoying without the addition of expensive apparatus.... Children sit on door-steps and on the pavement, they play in the gutter, they chase each other in the road, and dodge in and out of houses. It is evident that the School Board has not much power in the neighbourhood of the Dials. Public houses abound, and it is evident that whatever there may be a lack of in the Dials, there is no lack of money for drink.

Henry Mayhew in his *London Labour and the London Poor* (*c*.1861) noted that there was hardly an English tradesman in the area – they were all Irish. One man reported to Mayhew that a Roman Catholic of his acquaintance, who knew he was dying, declined to ask the priest to come to his lodgings in Seven Dials because they were so filthy – five men lived and worked in the same room as he. 'In many houses in Monmouth Street there is a system of sub-letting among the journeymen. In one room lodged a man and his wife (a laundress), four children and two single young men. The woman was actually delivered in this room whilst the men kept at their work – they never lost an hour's work.'

Almost certainly this concentration of Irish in Seven Dials was the result of the construction of New Oxford Street in 1847, which had obliterated the traditional and tightly packed Irish quarter in the St Giles Rookery. No attempt was made to rehouse the occupants of that area and they would simply have squeezed in as best they could just to the south. Endell Street was also constructed at the same time – a relatively spacious street, containing a number of public buildings, which again displaced housing in the area. The condition of Seven Dials improved with the construction of Charing Cross Road and Shaftesbury Avenue in the 1880s and by the twentieth century its trading nature was mainly of small household shops and craftsmen, with the occasional large firm such as the Combe and Delafield brewery (whose buildings still survive) in Shelton Street, and Comyn Ching in Monmouth Street, whose various premises, when redevelopment was being planned in the 1970s, were given the rather sinister sounding name of the Comyn Ching Triangle.

50. *An old clothes shop in Seven Dials. (From* Street Life in London, *published 1877).*

The Eastern Fringes

GREAT QUEEN STREET

The building of Great Queen Street began in the earliest years of the seventeenth century and by 1623 fifteen houses were completed. The first were on the north side of the street, their occupants having an uninterrupted view to the heights of north London. It was what commentators called 'a regular street', meaning straight, regulated and fairly uniform, much as those in the later Covent Garden scheme were to be. The houses were of brick and of sufficient status to attract good tenants, but why the street was built at that time – for it was then in an isolated location – is unclear. At its eastern end it ran into the then unbuilt Lincoln's Inn Fields; to the west Long Acre was still a field name with a track through it, and north and south were still largely agricultural. Only Drury Lane, to which Great Queen Street connected via a gate, had development of consequence. But the street's name – a specially procured tribute to James I's queen, Anne of Denmark – indicates its status. Indeed, it formed part of the route that James I took on his frequent travels from Whitehall, up through Long

52. *No. 4 Great Queen Street in 1904.*

51. *Nos 55-56 Great Queen Street in 1848. From a watercolour by J.W. Archer, 1846.*

Acre, then Great Queen Street and into what became Theobalds Road, to his Theobalds mansion in Hertfordshire. By 1658, according to Hollar's map of the area, the street was fully built up.

By the nineteenth century many of the traders in Great Queen Street were intimately connected with the coachbuilding firms of Long Acre. A directory of 1817 lists numerous premises devoted to the minutiae of the trade, such as ironmongery, harness makers, platers, breeches makers, bit makers etc.

Developers of the street included Sir Kenelm Digby, William Newton and John Parker, the last two commemorated in local street names; Newton was also responsible for the first buildings in Lincoln's Inn Fields, which stood in the same field as the eastern end of Great Queen Street. The physical relationship between Great Queen Street and Lincoln's Inn Fields today is now obscured by the wide intrusion of modern Kingsway. The houses that Newton built on the south side of Great Queen Street were of substance – one of them containing in its frontage a statue of Queen Henrietta Maria, consort of Charles I.

THE FREEMASONS

The site of the 'statue house' was the first to be acquired by the Freemasons in this street. In 1774 it was purchased by the Grand Lodge of Free and Accepted Masons; the premises comprised a house fronting Great Queen Street let to a paper stainer, and another, smaller, house to the rear which became the Freemasons' Tavern, with some of it fitted up as committee rooms for the Lodge. There were soon changes. The following year the architect Thomas Sandby demolished the old houses and built a Freemasons' Hall (or Temple), which was opened in 1776, and ten years later another Freemasons' Tavern was added. Adjoining buildings were gradually acquired. Conway House was demolished and rebuilt as additional premises by Sir John Soane in 1829. In 1863 two further houses and the tavern and hall were demolished to make way for a new Freemasons' Hall designed by F.P. Cockerell, which opened in 1866. The site of this building is now covered by the Connaught Rooms, though part of the facade of Cockerell's hall and his banqueting hall were retained in the new building.

53. Freemasons' Hall in 1811; from an engraving by S. Rawle after a drawing by I. Nixon.

54. Freemasons' Hall in 1866. From The Builder.

The absurdly pompous Freemasons' Hall which now dominates the western end of Great Queen Street, was designed by H.V. Ashley and F. Winton Newman, and completed in 1933.

On the other side of the street the business of Toye, Kenning and Spencer caters for the arcane ceremonies and insignias of the Freemasons. William Toye, a braid and lacemaker, is listed in the Old Ford Road in East London as a masonic supplier in 1880, while George Kenning, masonic publisher, had premises in Little Britain and Fleet Street before moving to Great Queen Street in the 1880s; a large part of his business during this century revolved around ribbons, military and otherwise. Richard Spencer sold masonic books in Great Queen Street.

Other masonic buildings included the Royal Masonic Institute for Boys at Nos 24-6, a similar institution for girls at Nos 30-31 and a masonic lodge at No. 27.

DRURY LANE

Drury Lane is one of the oldest roads in the Covent Garden area, known as the 'Via de Aldwych' on older maps and, possibly, was part of the settlement of *Lundenwic* (see pp7-8). It takes its name from Sir William Drury, who built a house at the southern end of the road during the reign of Elizabeth I. At that time the Strand was reached from Drury Lane only via a narrow alley, and the main southern exit from the Lane was through Wych Street, a narrow road that struck south-east down to the Strand (see ill. 7) to emerge by St Clement Danes. Drury's house was roughly at that junction of Drury Lane and Wych Street. The whole of the Wych Street area was demolished when Aldwych was constructed at the turn of this century.

Throughout the seventeenth century Drury Lane was a reasonably fashionable thoroughfare. The poet, John Donne, stayed at Drury House as a guest of Drury's son, Robert, and it was here that he had a vision of his wife 'with her hair hanging about her shoulders and a dead child in her arms' just at the time when his wife had been delivered of a stillborn child in Paris.

Drury House was rebuilt in the 1620s by Sir William Craven (and renamed Craven House), destroyed by

55. *Freemasons' Hall, 1956.*

56. *Craven House, at the junction of Drury Lane and Wych Street.*

fire and then rebuilt again. The grounds of Craven House, on the east side of Drury Lane, were developed for poor-class housing after 1723 and the old mansion was let out into tenements and inevitably deteriorated. Its site was taken to build the Olympic Theatre in 1805.

Pepys knew Drury Lane. He notes with dismay in his *Diary* two or three houses marked with the insignia of the Plague during 1665, but more happily in 1667 he records:

'To Westminster; in the way meeting many milk-maids with their garlands upon their pails, dancing with a fiddler before them; and saw pretty Nelly [Gwyn] standing at her lodgings door in Drury Lane in her smock-sleeves and bodice, looking upon one; she seemed a mighty pretty creature.'

The numerous courtyards on both sides of Drury Lane, and the adjacency of two theatres, brought down the status of the road. Steele described it as divided into 'ladyships', "over which matrons of known abilities preside".

Some of Drury Lane was photographed by members of an early photographic society in the 1880s, because of its old buildings and the likelihood of their demolition – see illustrations 57 and 58. A good stretch of the road was redeveloped for model housing as the slums were taken down.

57. Drury Lane in the 1880s.

58. Drury Lane in the 1880s, looking south to St Mary-le-Strand.

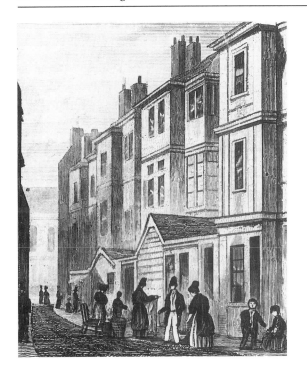

59. *(Top left) Drury Court, off Drury Lane.*

60. *(Bottom left) Parker Street; drawing by Fred Adcock.*

61. *(Above) Drury Lane, by T.G. Fraser.*

62. *Kemble Street, by T.G. Fraser.*

63. *White Horse Yard, off Drury Lane, by T.G. Fraser.*

64. *Little Wild Street (now Keeley Street) looking north-east in 1906.*

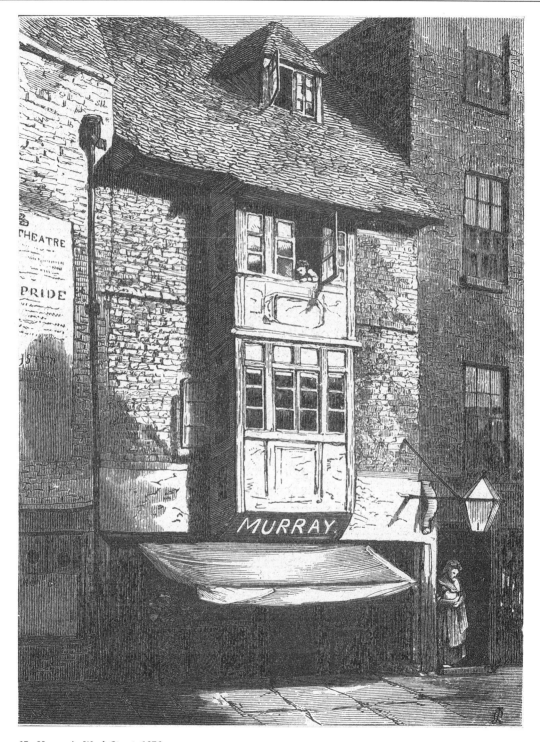

65. Houses in Wych Street, 1876.

66. *A coachmaker's premises in Long Acre, 1870.*

A Street of Coaches and Printers

Long Acre never was an acre – it was a narrow seven-acre strip north of the convent garden and the word 'acre' was probably used in the earlier sense meaning field, or else it represented a strip in a much larger open field. As we have seen (p8), it came into the possession of the Bedford Estate once it had been acquired by the Crown from Westminster Abbey and the road itself eventually marked the boundary between the Bedford Estate and that of the Mercers' Company to its north. The street was laid out about 1615, the houses on the south side having grounds that extended to the wall that had been built north of what is now Floral Street (see ill. 2) and within which the nucleus of the Covent Garden estate was laid out. Thus these premises had extensive gardens which later that century were useful when the trade of coachmaking became concentrated in Long Acre.

It was stipulated when the plots were let out, that any houses built were to be 'substantiallie and stronglie [built] and in a convenient decent and comelie forme, and three stories in height (yf not above)....' By the middle of the century Howell, in his *Londinopolis*, was able to describe it as 'a spacious fair street'. Long Acre was of some personal interest to the King – as we have seen (pp43-4) it was part of the route that James I habitually took to travel to his country house at Theobalds. As early as 1616 a Sir William Slingsby (who is commemorated in a short turning off Long Acre) had to eat humble pie when he conceded that the king was displeased 'about the direction of a way which has been made by him in Long Acre' and proffered 'entire submission' in the matter..

Coaches became popular during the mid-seventeenth century – Pepys, who bought a second-hand coach in the City as his financial fortunes improved, brought it to Long Acre to be refinished in a style which he could afford. Hollar's map of 1658 shows what appears to be large stables, probably livery stables, on the south side of Long Acre, with a substantial courtyard at the rear, and Lacy's map of Covent Garden in 1673 names these premises as

Salisbury's stables. By the beginning of the nine-teenth century the majority of premises in the street were used by traders in the coachmaking industry, as were those in adjacent roads such as Mercer Street. Ruskin records that as a boy he came here with his parents to choose a coach to use on a continental tour.

This specialty lasted into the motor car age and eventually was of necessity transformed into car build-ing. In 1916, for example, many of the premises were taken by car salesmen, or body builders and repair-ers. Fiat Motors were on the south side by Langley Court, Daimler and Mercedes were on the north side, next to General Motors, while Blériot Aeroplanes (Nos 57-9) and Merryweather fire engines (No. 63) were also present.

ODHAMS PRESS

As car making disappeared from Long Acre printing took its place. This was represented largely by the company called Odhams Press, which had begun in 1894 under the ownership of the Odhams brothers in Floral Street – their father had a similar business in Burleigh Street. At a time when the machinery was antiquated and business at a low ebb they were persuaded to take on, as office boy, Julius Salter Elias who, within a year, had taken over as manager.

68. Julius Salter Elias (1873-1946). He was created Viscount Southwood in 1937.

67. The Odhams printing works at Nos. 19-24 Floral Street (then called Hart Street). The business was founded in 1894.

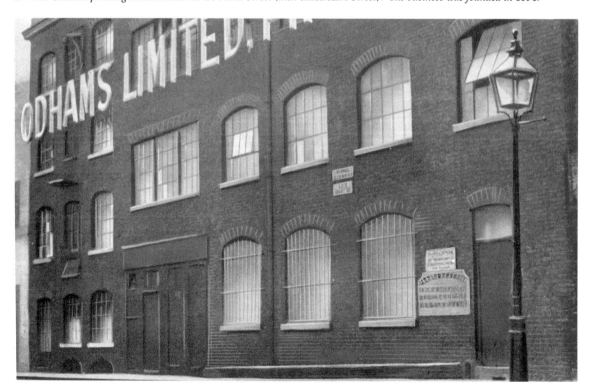

69. Odhams offices in the old Queen's Theatre in 1927; drawing by Hanslip Fletcher.

Elias was an obsessive and meticulous worker. He realised that the only way to make the company prosperous was to obtain magazine work so that they had regular turnover and income instead of the haphazard expectations that were the lot of jobbing printers. They were, after all, within reach of many journals in the Fleet Street and Covent Garden area.

His persistence paid off. Publications of all kinds – *Physical Culture, Racing Pigeon, The Family Doctor* and *Vanity Fair* – were printed in Floral Street. By 1906 Odhams needed more space for already much of their work was printed at another firm of printers. They moved into the old Queen's Theatre at 93 Long Acre, a building with splendid Ionic columns, which they shared with paper merchants, with a seed merchant in the royal circle, and contractors to the Post Office in the pit. Gradually Odhams began to fill the building.

The turning point in the firm's fortunes came with the contract to print the magazine *John Bull*. This weekly journal became notorious in publishing history. It was founded by a jingoist and flamboyant MP

called Horatio Bottomley, whose lifestyle was a scandal and a subject of envy. He dabbled in many things, sometimes dubious things, and his charisma persuaded people to part with their investments. *John Bull* was an instant success. Its style was racy, its contents attracted writs by the score, and it set out to expose corruption wherever it could imagine it.

The trouble as far as Odhams were concerned was that Bottomley did not pay his bills and eventually the company took over the magazine to safeguard their money. Circulation reached a remarkable 1,700,000 copies, but once Bottomley had departed it plummeted to 300,000. Elias persevered, however, and pushed it up to a million again.

In the meantime he took on other publications and, with much success, invented his own so as to fill his presses. He began *Ideal Home*, and developed *Picturegoer* as cinema became popular. He printed *The People* newspaper, then on hard times, he bought *Sporting Life*, and later on took on the *Daily Herald* in association with the Trades Union Congress. This

70. *J. Davy & Sons 'Dryden Press' at 137 Long Acre. Note the bust of Dryden, one time resident of Long Acre, above the shop front.*

newspaper, begun as a strike sheet in 1911, became massively popular until the late 1950s and then declined: its descendant today is *The Sun*, whose politics and journalistic approach are vastly different.

The Odhams factories in Long Acre were gradually superseded by another in Watford and the offices also departed. The old firm are commemorated today by Odhams Walk on the corner of Long Acre and Neal Street, the site of an old printing factory.

HAZELL, WATSON AND VINEY

Another famous Covent Garden printer – like Odham's, now submerged in conglomerate ownership – was Hazell, Watson and Viney. This firm's prosperity began in 1851 when a printer called George Watson obtained the contract to print the *Band of Hope Review*, a temperance magazine at a time when the cause was a burgeoning one. In order to take it on, Watson bought a steam-driven printing machine which was installed at the firm's premises, then in Hatton Garden. For the same publisher Watson went on to print *The British Workman*, another didactic magazine, which was influential in the movement to obtain an early-closing day to ease the exploited conditions of shop workers and a day of rest for both cabbies and their horses.

Watson moved his office to 52 Long Acre in 1901. The company had a number of diversifications, such as the agency to sell what was then a famous pen nib, and part ownership of Letts diaries. Hazell's had a large factory at Aylesbury, just as Odham's had their main plant in Watford, and it was here that Hazell's developed their reputation for printing colour magazines. It was they who had the contract for *Good Housekeeping* (1922), *Harper's Bazaar* (1929), *Connoisseur* (1934) and later they formed close trade bonds with both Pearson's and Newnes (see p117).

71 The head office of Hazell, Watson & Viney at 52 Long Acre. The entrance to the works was in Floral Street at the rear, opposite the Royal Opera House stage door.

72. *Tom's Coffee House in Russell Street, 1857; watercolour by T.H. Shepherd.*

A Pleasurable Life

COFFEE HOUSES

The rage for coffee-houses began after the Restoration in 1660 and was at its height in the eighteenth century. Some were hardly more than business premises in which traders in common commodities gathered, swapped news and made deals. Some, such as Lloyd's, developed into institutions. Around St Paul's and its churchyard the customers were clerical and bookish, since much of London's publishing was centred in that area. In the West End many of the clientele were also the rakes who joined the men's clubs around Pall Mall. Those in the Strand and Covent Garden area catered particularly for people in theatre and journalism. As conduits for news and opinion coffee houses were viewed suspiciously by the authorities, who feared sedition. Charles II attempted a rash suppres-

sion of them, which failed ignominiously, and by 1698 it is estimated that there were 2,000 in London, occupying more premises and paying more rent than any other trade. As John Ashton noted in his *Social Life in the Reign of Queen Anne* (1897), a coffee house was 'the centre of news, the lounge of the idler, the rendezvous for appointments, mart for business men.'

Numerous coffee-houses existed in Covent Garden, especially around the Piazza itself, but three of the best-known in London vied for custom in Russell Street – Tom's and Button's, with Will's on the corner of the same street with Bow Street.

Tom's Coffee House was on the first floor of No. 17 (a bookseller occupied the ground floor). It was founded by Captain Thomas West in 1700, and he remained the proprietor until 1722 when, apparently driven to extreme by gout, he threw himself to his death from a second floor window. It was in that year that Macky in his *Journey through England* wrote that 'After the play the best company generally go to Tom's and Will's Coffee Houses near adjoining, where there is playing at Picket, and the best of conversation till midnight. Here you will see blue and green ribbons and Stars sitting familiarly, and talking with the same freedom as if they had left their quality and degrees of distance at home.' Macky was particularly impressed by the mixture of classes at Tom's where

73. *The Caledonian Coffee House, formerly Button's Coffee House, Russell Street, 1857; watercolour by T.H. Shepherd.*

74. *Joseph Addison; from a painting by Dahl.*

75. No. 21 Russell Street, former home of Will's Coffee House; drawn by Fredk. Adcock.

they enjoyed the 'universal liberty of Speech of the English Nation'. Patrons there included Dr Johnson, Sir Joshua Reynolds and George Steevens, the Shakespearian commentator. Tom's became a private club in 1768, where for an annual fee of a guinea 'nearly seven hundred of the nobility, foreign ministers, gentry and geniuses of the age' used the card room and other facilities.

Button's Coffee House, on the south side of Russell Street, had a short life. It was opened in 1712 and appears to have closed in the 1730s. This was founded by Daniel Button, a former servant of the Countess of Warwick, whose second husband, Joseph Addison, set him up in business. Addison therefore felt it appropriate to use the coffee-house as an unofficial headquarters and publishing base. It was at Button's that he erected a letter box in the shape of a lion's head, in which people could post contributions to *The Guardian*, a journal of Addison and Steele's, which succeeded the better-known *Spectator*. This famous piece of furniture later found its way to the Duke of Bedford's Woburn Abbey.

76. The 'Rustic Smoking Promenade' at Gliddon's Cigar Divan, 42 King Street; drawn and etched by Benson Hill.

77. *John Dryden.*

78. *Rule's Restaurant, Maiden Lane.*

The death of Addison and then of Steele led to a fall in Button's fortunes and he died, penurious and in receipt of parish relief, in 1731.

Will's began as a tavern but in 1671 its owner, William Urwin, turned it into a coffee house which was fortunate to obtain the regular custom of John Dryden, then regarded as the principal literary lion in London. So frequent a customer and so revered was he that Dryden's regular seat upstairs by the fire in winter, and his chair on the balcony overlooking Bow Street in summer, were reserved for him by common assent. Alexander Pope as a young man persuaded devotees of the place to take him there so that he could view Dryden, but Pope describes him as 'a plump man with a down look, and not very conversible'. Jonathan Swift thought the place dull as did Ned Ward writing in 1703.

At No. 42 King Street in the eighteenth century was a smoking 'divan', one of a number in London which were basically men's clubs, a place to smoke, talk and read newspapers, but without the membership requirement.

Until recent times Covent Garden, with a few exceptions, has not been noted for its restaurants. Many of the appropriate age bracket speak fondly of the Boulestin at the corner of Southampton Street and Henrietta Street. But the most famous – and surviving – establishment is Rule's in Maiden Lane, possibly the

79. *Advertisement for Hewitt's Hotel for Gentlemen, previously the Old Hummums Turkish bath.*

oldest reataurant in London. It claims ancestry back to 1798 and it certainly had premises at Nos. 36-8 in 1828. The present building at Nos. 34-5 was built in the 1870s, but only No. 35 was used by Rule's until the restaurant was extended in the 1960s. On the first floor is a curtained alcove in which Edward VII entertained the actress, Lily Langtry, their meetings carefully managed by discreet staff and staircases. Dickens and Thackeray were frequent diners at Rule's.

BAGNIOS AND BAWDS

A writer in 1776 noted that Covent Garden Piazza was 'the great square of Venus, and its purlieus are crowded with the votaries of this goddess.... The jelly-houses are now become the resort of abandoned rakes and shameless prostitutes. These and the taverns afford an ample supply of provisions for the flesh; while others abound for the consummation of the desires which are thus excited. For this vile end the bagnios and lodging-houses are near at hand.' He went on: 'One would imagine that all the prostitutes of the Kingdom had pitched upon this blessed neighbourhood... For here are lewd women in sufficient numbers to people a mighty colony.' It was beneath the portico houses that James Boswell in 1763 walked up and down summoning courage to pick himself a woman from among the many.

A number of coffee-houses and taverns were little more than brothels, but there were other establishments – bagnios – that trod a fine line between respectability and disreputability, much as sauna establishments do today. The oldest bagnio in the

Piazza was the Hummums, opened in 1683, originally on the south-west corner of Russell Street by the Piazza, a place for 'sweating and bathing': in effect a Turkish bath. The price for bathing was 5/6d, for two in one room 8/- and the price for an overnight stay 10/-. This became a respectable place by all accounts, but only after an announcement in 1701 which declared that the place 'having for several years been neglected and abused by those persons that had the care and management of them, whereby several persons of quality have been disgusted, and have left off coming thither to sweat and bathe as formerly: This is to give notice that the said Hummums are now in possession of others, who have refitted the same and rectified all those neglects and abuses....' The place eventually became a hotel at which Dr Wolcot and Alfred, Lord Tennyson stayed.

But there were plenty more bagnios, some of them the resort of prostitutes, which were denoted, one writer asserts, by a bunch of grapes hung up outside. One belonged to a lady known as 'Hell Fire Stanhope', formerly a mistress of Sir Francis Dashwood of the well-known Hell Fire Club. Another bagnio owner in the Piazza was Mother Douglas who was portrayed in one of Hogarth's prints depicting riotous London.

Another place that went down in the world was the King's Bagnio in Long Acre, near to Conduit Court, which was established in 1682. It was described a year later as a 'stately edifice, of an oval figure, in length 45 feet, and in breadth 35 feet, in which there are several round glasses fixt to let in light, which are much larger, and no fewer in number than those of the Royal Bagnio.'

80. Scene in the Cider Cellars, Maiden Lane, well known for its company and musical evenings.

81. *The Lamb and Flag in Rose Street, 1968, one of Covent Garden's best known public houses.*

82. *Another view of the the Cock and Magpie in Drury Lane. This tavern, which was later converted to a bookshop, was on the west side of Drury Lane, at the southern end, opposite Craven House.*

83. The Bird in Hand, at the corner of Long Acre and Conduit Court.

Prostitution was an inevitable part of Covent Garden since attendance at the two theatres at the time was often an introduction to it. Legions of prostitutes patrolled the pavements outside the theatres and the vestibules inside, spilling over to the bars and coffee houses on the Piazza, Russell Street and Floral Street. Macklin Street, then called Lewknor's Lane, was notorious in the eighteenth century and is mentioned in *The Beggar's Opera* as a street from where prostitutes were being procured for the amusement of Macheath. Sir Roger L'Estrange, writing in 1715, refers to it as being a 'rendezvous and nursery for lewd women first resorted to by the Roundheads'. Nor was this confined to the eighteenth century. A tenant of Floral Street near its junction with Bow Street complained to the parish vestry in 1844 that he had 'numerous Brothels situated around my house'. Two years earlier there were complaints about a brothel in Exeter Street, run by a Mrs Crutchley, 'where scenes of the grossest infamy are daily exposed. The house appears to be the resort of women of the lowest description whose screams throughout the greater part of the night keep the neighbourhood in a constant state of annoyance. Cries of murder have made it necessary frequently to call in the Police. Women in a state of almost perfect nudity and drunkenness are constantly exposing themselves in the yard of the said premises.'

THE TAVERNS

One of the oldest of Covent Garden's many taverns is the Nag's Head in James Street, depicted on a map of 1673, though the present neo-Jacobean building was erected in 1900. The Lamb and Flag in the minute Rose Street appears to be very old, outside and in; it was probably rebuilt in the early eighteenth century, but there is no record of it being a public house until 1772, when it was called the Cooper's Arms – it took its present name in 1833. It stands by a convoluted passageway built to connect Long Acre to King Street before the construction of Garrick Street in the 1860s made it superfluous. (At the same time, Floral Street, which previously terminated east of Rose Street, was extended into Garrick Street). Rose Street had a particularly bad reputation both for its brothels and insanitary condition. As originally built in the 1630s, the houses were 'fitt for mechaniks only and persons of meane quallite'. It was the scene, in 1679, of an attack on the poet, Dryden, described in the contemporary *Mercurius Domesticus*:

Mr Dryden.... was set upon.... by three persons, who calling him rogue, and son of a whore, knockt him down, and dangerously wounded him, but upon his crying out murther, they made their escape; it is conceived that they had their pay beforehand, and designed not to rob him...'

It has been suggested, in view of the fact that Dryden was not robbed, that the attack was at the behest of the Earl of Rochester, a reprisal for a satire on him which he claimed had been written by Dryden. This incident is recorded on the ceiling of the passageway beside the Lamb and Flag, which places the blame for the attack elsewhere:

'Stay traveller rest and refresh yrself in this ancient tavern in whose walls so many great figures of the past have taken their ease. Here often sat the immortal Charles Dickens & his friends, poor Samuel Butler and the wits and gallants of the restoration. Hither resorted the Bucks and Dandies to witness prize fights & cock mains, while hard by was enacted the notorious Rose Alley Ambuscade in Decr 1679 when the poet Dryden was almost done to death at the instance of Louise de Keroualle, mistress of Charles II.'

The Cider Cellars in Maiden Lane were renowned for their musical evenings. Thackeray described them thus:

Healthy country tradesmen and farmers in London for their business, came and recreated themselves with the jolly singing and suppers at the Back Kitchen; squads of young apprentices and assistants – the shutters being closed over the scene of their labours – came hither, for fresh air doubtless. Dashing young medical students, gallant, clashing, what is called loudly dressed and must it be owned? somewhat dirty, came here, smoking and drinking and vigorously applauding the songs; young University bucks were to be found here, too, with that indescribable simper which is only learned at the knees of Alma Mater, and handsome young guardsmen and florid bucks from the St James' Street clubs.

84. *No. 43 King Street, when used as a coffee house and hotel. W.C. Evans obtained a lease of the 'Grand Hotel' in the 1840s and built an addition to the basement to house a music hall (see Illustration 141)*

In the same street, the Bedford Head (now called the Maple Leaf) was here in the early eighteenth century and was probably used by Voltaire, who lived a few doors away for a time. A club, whose members included Hogarth, Fielding and Goldsmith, met here.

Both the Globe and the Marquis of Anglesey in Bow Street occupy sites used by victuallers in the later seventeenth century. Around the corner, in Catherine Street, the attractive Opera Tavern, built in 1879 by George Treacher, replaces a public house called Sheridan Knowles after a now largely forgotten Irish playwright whose works were performed at the Theatre Royal opposite.

In King Street the Essex Serpent was known as such in 1743, and is thought to derive its name from a report from Saffron Walden of a sighting of a 'Monstrous Serpent which hath divers times been seen at a Parish called Henham-on-the-Mount.' Along the road, where Garrick Street joins, the Round House, formerly a hotel called Petter's, is a reminder of the parish lock-up, and in New Row the White Swan is built on the site of a house which was occupied by Lady Stanhope and the Countess of Chesterfield in the seventeenth century.

THE GARRICK

The Garrick Club was founded in 1831 by the Duke of Sussex, mainly for patrons of drama. The present clubhouse in Garrick Street was designed by Frederick Marrable, and was the principal building in Garrick Street when it was formed in the 1860s. The nucleus of the Club's marvellous collection of paintings, including portraits by Zoffany, Kneller and Lely, was purchased from an early member, the actor Charles Mathews the Elder.

The Club originally met at No. 35 King Street. It was here that a famous falling-out between Thackeray and Dickens took place. This stemmed from an article about Thackeray, written by another Club member, Edward Yates, which appeared in 1858. Thackeray considered it slanderous and demanded an apology, and upon being refused he complained to the committee of the Club. A later general meeting of members called on Yates to apologise, but Dickens took his part and, indeed, thought that the Club had no right to interfere in the matter.

The alienation between the two writers continued virtually until Thackeray's death in 1863, when the two met on the steps of the Athenaeum and spontaneously shook hands.

85. The Garrick Club in Garrick Street.

Legal Innovations

THE BOW STREET OFFICE

The system of magistrates courts which now operates in England, and the police force which serves them, both stem largely from Bow Street in Covent Garden.

By the eighteenth century crime was rife in London and the population virtually unprotected. An inefficient system of watching and patrolling, grudgingly paid for by thrifty parishes, was compounded by usually corrupt justices who accepted bribes in the course of their duties. It was not uncommon for an 'unpaid' magistrate to make £1,000 a year from his post. His clerk and his constables might also be involved in the corruption so that it was possible for the well-known criminal, Jonathan Wild, to organise profitable robberies with the full connivance of the petty judiciary. The scandal was known by the authorities and by Londoners, as the appreciation of John Gay's *The Beggar's Opera*, which exposed it, showed. Some public figures, such as Sir John Gonson,

attempted reform – he was chairman of the Westminster magistrates and is depicted in Hogarth's *Harlot's Progress* leading a group of his officers into a brothel to arrest the occupants.

Thomas de Veil, the son of a Huguenot cleric, was, however, the first prominent instrument of change. In 1740 he set up his magistrate's office on the west side of Bow Street just south of Covent Garden Theatre – the site is now taken by former market buildings. Together with the house next door, it remained a court house until the present court was built in 1880 on the opposite side of the road.

Though de Veil was himself a 'trading justice', it was known that he took only what was considered fair profit for the time and kept accounts of what he took. He seems to have been respected for his impartiality in dispensing justice and by the time of his death in 1747 the Bow Street office had acquired a unique status among magistrates courts.

Two years later the unlikely personage of Henry Fielding, novelist and playwright, became magistrate at Bow Street. It was the production of a Fielding satire on the Walpole administration in 1736 that led

86. *Thomas de Veil.*

87. *A hearing at the Bow Street magistrates court, with Sir John Fielding presiding.*

88. *Bow Street magistrates court, 1825; watercolour by J. Winston.*

89. *Interior of the magistrates court, Bow Street; from an aquatint by Pugin and Rowlandson, published 1808.*

90. Sir John Fielding.

precipitately to the introduction of an Act of Parliament which made it illegal for any play to be staged without the prior permission of the Lord Chamberlain – oppressive legislation which still pertained till recent times. Fielding abandoned play writing in such an atmosphere and in 1737 entered Middle Temple to study law and after 1740 became a circuit justice. It was due to the influence of an old schoolfriend with the Duke of Bedford that Fielding was appointed to the Bow Street court which served Westminster.

In his five years as magistrate here Fielding consolidated de Veil's earlier reputation for the Court and gave much thought and energy to the causes and remedies of the general lawlessness of the day.

Whatever Fielding might have wanted to do in the matter of policing, especially to quell riotous occasions, he was hampered by the lack of an effective force. In 1749 at Bow Street he formed a small, but permanent, nucleus of constables who were unpaid but entitled to a share of any reward money received for the apprehension of criminals. It was an unofficial arrangement and one that did not endear him to the public which assumed it was yet another way he had devised to deal in stolen goods.

Fielding's blind half-brother John was also appointed a Westminster magistrate in 1750, after several years of helping in the Bow Street office. After Henry's death in 1754, John took over and it was he that formed the Bow Street Runners, a small force of detectives, which could be claimed as the ancestor of the Metropolitan Police Force. John Fielding had less charm than his elder brother, but he had even more diligence. Despite his handicap (he had gone blind at about the age of 19), he expanded the activities of his court and was prominent in some of the better-known charities of the day. He took practical steps to control

91. Model of John Townsend, a Bow Street Runner.

92. A force of 'Peelers'. The location is unknown.

93. *The new courthouse in Bow Street, 1879, designed by John Taylor. From* The Builder, *21 June 1879.*

the dissipating spread of ginshops and brothels, evolved schemes for the welfare of young prostitutes, and worked with Jonas Hanway in the Marine Society, which trained young homeless boys in skills that would enable them to work at sea.

In 1762 he published a *Plan for Preventing Robberies within Twenty Miles of London,* which recommended the overhaul of the police force and justice system. Little was implemented though Fielding made good headway in persuading parishes to introduce far more street lighting to make the streets safer, and he seems to have begun the practice of having the lights on the pavement, rather than attached to houses.

There was a great deal of disorder in London in the 1760s, much of it related to the protracted fight by the flamboyant John Wilkes to be accepted as a Member of Parliament, and the London constables were quite unable to cope with the numerous demonstrations and riots that occurred throughout the years to the end of the decade. Fielding was the chief witness before a government committee in 1770 set up to discuss policing the capital, and he once again pressed for a centralised authority which would employ the constables instead of them being under the aegis of local parishes. He also wanted magistrates to be paid so that they could be financially sustained without the aid of bribes.

Not much had improved by 1780 when the anti-Catholic Gordon Riots turned London upside down. People were murdered, many buildings destroyed and damaged, including the Bow Street office, and fifty thousand people besieged Parliament, there to pelt and beat Members.

Fielding died in 1780 and despite the severity of the riots of that year only gradual improvements were made. Paid magistrates were introduced in 1792 but it was not until the successful introduction of a River Police to curb theft in the London docks that the time became right for the formation of a police force for the streets of London. This resulted from a Bill introduced by Sir Robert Peel, which gained assent in 1829. The new force, some of whom are shown in Illustration 92, were usually called Peelers in his honour.

In the meantime the Bow Street office was still progressive. Under a new magistrate, Richard Ford, who was also the supposed husband of the actress, Dorothy Jordan, and financially involved with the Theatre Royal, mounted patrols became a familiar feature of London – they were the first police force to wear a uniform.

Once the Metropolitan Police had been established in 1829 Bow Street's central role in policing was removed to Scotland Yard, but it continued to be the principal court for Westminster.

The Making of the Market

A MARKET BUILDING

Illustration 3 shows the extent of Covent Garden market in *c*.1717. It occupied the southern part of the railed-off square, with some permanent sheds to the edge and some covered stalls to the centre. It was not, at least if Sutton Nicholls' print is accurate, a large operation, but in views of 1751 and 1761 the trading has extended across the whole of the Piazza, though the temporary shed structures were still on the southern part only. By the beginning of the nineteenth century Covent Garden market had grown to a substantial affair selling not merely fruit and vegetables but other items such as crockery. The Bedfords, after a period of farming out the tolls, were then in direct receipt of them and there were numerous disputes because the original charter had left so many areas for contention. An Act that the Bedford family had obtained in 1813 allowed some of the worst features to be remedied, such as the removal of obstructions, and the regular cleaning of the square, but the question of tolls was still not resolved satisfactorily to the various parties. It was time for change.

Change came in the form of a proper market building. The Bedford Estate manager chose Charles Fowler to design it, for he and many others were impressed by Fowler's recently opened Hungerford Market on the site of today's Charing Cross station. The Covent Garden market buildings, which were erected while trade continued, were substantially what we see today, except that there was no roof. They consisted of three parallel ranges of shops, offices and cellars, within which provision was made for a suitable number of taverns. Traders positioned themselves for the most part where they had been before – potato merchants to the south, alongside herb shops and better-class fruiterers, beans and peas were to the east and so on.

The coming of the railways, which dramatically increased the population of London, caught Covent Garden market out. It wasn't near any main line station, excepting Charing Cross, which was mainly for passenger traffic, and this meant that the greater volume of fruit and vegetables coming in to London by rail had to be loaded on to waggons for road transportation to Covent Garden – a similar problem applied to Billingsgate, whereas Smithfield, when it was rebuilt in the 1850s, had its own station beneath. The situation was not improved in Covent Garden when Hungerford Market, which also handled fruit and vegetables, was closed in the 1850s to make way for Charing Cross station. So, congestion prevailed in the narrow streets around the market and access, as we have seen (p17), was decidedly restricted. So desperate was the Bedford Estate to remedy this that it contributed to the construction of Garrick Street in the 1860s, and also paid for road improvements south of the market.

Dickens, inevitably, was on hand to describe the scenes of chaos at Covent Garden:

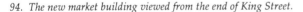

94. The new market building viewed from the end of King Street.

95. *'The Terrace of the the Bedford Conservatories, being one of the Improvements in the New Market Covent Garden',
published 1831.*

All night long on the great main roads the rumble of the
heavy waggons seldom ceases and before daylight the
market is crowded. The very unloading of these waggons
is in itself a wonder, and the wall-like regularity with which
cabbages, cauliflowers, turnips are built up to a height of
some 12ft is nothing short of marvellous. Between 5 and 6
o'clock the light traps of the greengrocers of the metropolis
rattle up, and all the streets around the market become
thronged with their carts, while the costermongers come in
in immense numbers. If it be a summer-time flowers as well
as fruits are sold at the early markets. Then there are
hundreds of women and girls among the crowd, purchas-
ing bunches of roses, violets and other flowers, and then
sitting down on the steps of the church, or of the houses
round the market, dividing the large bunches into smaller
ones, or making those pretty button-hole bouquets in which
our London flower-girls can now fairly hold their own in
point of taste with those of France or Italy.... On each side
of the main avenue (within the central market building) are
enclosed squares and here the wholesale fruit market is
carried on. In winter there are thousands of boxes of
oranges, hundreds of sacks of nuts, boxes of Hamburg
grapes and of French winter pears, barrels of bright American apples. At ten o'clock the sale begins; auctioneers stand
on boxes and while the more expensive fruits are purchased
by the West-end fruiterers, the cheaper are briskly bid for
by the costermongers.

NEW HALLS

Most likely, if the new market buildings had been
constructed twenty years later they would have been
entirely different. Advantage would have been taken
of new building techniques using iron and glass, so
splendidly demonstrated in the Crystal Palace for the
Great Exhibition in 1851, and the market would have
had a large open span instead of being divided into
the traditional, but restrictive, avenues that Fowler
designed.

The first use of iron and glass in Covent Garden
actually occurred in 1860, when the Floral Hall was
built, not by the Bedford Estate, but by the management of Covent Garden Theatre. The theatre had
burned down in 1856 and its owners took the opportunity, when planning a new building, to take a lease
on some land adjoining and there erected a private
flower market, called the Floral Hall. The architect for
this, as with the rebuilt (present) theatre, was E.M.
Barry – a remarkable pair of buildings in entirely
diverse building styles. But as Robert Thorne has
pointed out, the arched construction and the dome,
which were at the heart of the Floral Hall's attractive-
ness (sadly, the dome was lost in a fire in 1956), were
inserted at the insistence of the Bedford Estate.

The Floral Hall was, however, a commercial failure
– probably because of the competition of the Bedford
flower market, noted below, which opened at about

96. *The Floral Hall, built by the management of Covent Garden Theatre, and designed by E.M. Barry.*

97. *Interior of the Floral Hall as proposed in 1857. From the* Illustrated London News.

the same time, and in 1887 the Floral Hall was bought by the Bedfords and converted to a foreign fruit market.

Extension beyond the Bedfords' original market area first occurred in 1860 when the Estate erected a temporary flower market on the south-east corner of the Piazza – this quickly became a permanent feature, was rebuilt in 1870-2 and further extended to Bow Street in 1885. These buildings now house the London Transport Museum and the Theatre Museum.

Further improvements came with the erection by William Cubitt of a roof over the main market building and the construction of a Foreign Flower market south of the Piazza, which became known as the Jubilee Hall – this was opened in 1904.

SELLING THE MARKET

Criticism of the Bedford Estate's ownership and management of Covent Garden grew as the nineteenth century lengthened. The Estate, far from reaping praise as it added new buildings to cope with the trade, was accused of misuse of its power over the traders. Not only did the Estate exact tolls within the market buildings themselves, but it did so in the streets as market business inevitably spilled over. With a small exception, Covent Garden was the only

market in London in private hands and with the growing enthusiasm for municipalisation, which culminated in the creation of the London County Council in 1889, the Bedfords' 'tax on food' was seen as iniquitous.

By that time too many voices had been raised criticising the location of the market. Even in the nineteenth century it was considered badly sited and, as it functioned all through the night, it drew traffic into an area where a large residential area was trying to sleep. It was a magnet for casual workers and scavengers and, because some public houses were open all night to cater for market people, a notorious place for getting drunk when other pubs had closed. The Bedfords were advised to sell out while the going was good, for almost anyone could have foreseen that the market would one day be relocated outside the central area and placed in the hands of another authority.

The Duke of Bedford had, as Thorne points out, indicated that he was willing to sell to the Metropolitan Board of Works as early as 1874, but the Board and the City declined to take the market on. In the end the Bedfords went into negotiations with a private buyer, H. Mallaby Deeley, a land speculator, for the sale of both the market and the estate surrounding it. The proposed deal was never consummated and the Bedfords turned to a consortium of businessmen led by Sir Joseph Beecham (the pill manufacturer and father of the future Sir Thomas Beecham). War intervened and Sir Joseph died in 1916, but the negotiations were revived and the estate was sold in 1918 to the newly-formed Covent Garden Estate Company, the majority of which was owned by Thomas Beecham and his brother Henry.

This sale did not, of course, solve anything. The market was still congested and crowded – so much so that at a public hearing one of the main traders, George Monro, suggested that the church and the opera house be removed so that the market could be extended. This was hardly a surprising statement from the firm which drove a carriageway through the Palladian gem, No. 43 King Street, so that lorries could reach the yard at the back of the building.

For all the hue and cry after the Bedfords and their successors, no credit redounds on London municipal authorities. They had declined to take on the market in 1874 and continued to be reluctant until 1961 when the Covent Garden Market Authority was established. Its first recommendation was to relocate the market to Beckton, East London, but this proved unattractive to the traders and workers themselves, the majority of whom came from south London. A site at Nine Elms was chosen instead and the market moved there in 1973.

Propping up the Poor

The conjunction of the slums of the St Giles' Rookery, Seven Dials and the promise of casual labour afforded by Covent Garden market inevitably brought the poor to the area, and in their wake the missions to ease their lives. Endell Street, carved out in the 1840s as a new road through slum property, contained the institutional side of poor relief. At the top end were the baths and washhouses run by the two parishes of St Giles-in-the-Fields and St George, Bloomsbury, superseded nowadays by the Oasis leisure complex. Across the road the St Giles' National Schools were built, a splendid Gothic building designed by E.M. Barry, who thus has three buildings in the area – the others being the Royal Opera House and the Floral Hall –

each in different architectural styles. On the day this school opened it had 900 pupils, but had a playground only 40ft square.

South of the baths on the same side was the St Giles' parish workhouse, which was demolished in the 1970s. Other official establishments were the Strand (later Westminster) Relieving Office, where handouts were made to the impoverished, at 15/16 Henrietta Street, a building that stretched into Maiden Lane at the rear; until recently at least, a stained glass window inside the building contained the initials of the Strand Union.

The London County Council opened a lodging house in Parker Street in 1893, but its main hostel accommodation was Bruce House in Kemble Street, built in 1906. Together with a lodging house in Deptford, these constituted the only such places provided by the LCC in London, since much of the

98. The interior of the boys' school room in the St Giles' National Schools at the northern end of Endell Street. The building still survives.

99. *The Baths and Washhouses of the parishes of St Giles-in-the-Fields and St George's Bloomsbury, 1853. The architects were Baly Pownall. The building has been superseded by the Oasis leisure complex.*

100. *The Borough of Holborn workhouse in Endell Street.*

101. *The architect, Sir James Pennethorne (1801-71), who was responsible for the creation of Endell Street. Though the architect of a number of fine London buildings, he is now best remembered for his work on improvement schemes. In 1826 he was involved in the relaying out of the streets at the west end of the Strand, and later he laid out Endell Street, New Oxford Street, Cranbourne Street and Commercial Street. He was also responsible for earlier plans for Garrick Street, Southwark Street and Old Street.*

102. *The St Giles' National Schools, Endell Street. The architect was E.M. Barry.*

103. A London County Council lodging house in Parker Street.

responsibility for housing single men in these circumstances was shouldered by Rowton Houses.

The two parishes of St Giles and St George also built almshouses in Smarts Place, but the main housing for the poor in Covent Garden was provided by Peabody – in Drury Lane and Bedfordbury – and the Society for Improving the Conditions of the Labouring Classes, with buildings in Wild Court and Macklin Street, and some renovated older dwellings in Parker Street. The area of the Peabody estate in Drury Lane was one of the worst in London. In Wych Street alone lived thousands of people, entire families in one room, five or six to a bed with very primitive facilities. In Bedfordbury, which George Sala described as a 'devious, slimey little reptile of a place', over 2,000 people lived in the slums of the 1870s. About 800 were displaced in the rebuilding and as many were housed, though it is unlikely that they were usually the same people.

There were several Christian missions also. The St

104. The cubicle bedrooms in the Parker Street lodging house.

105. *Among the interesting buildings in the new Endell Street was this stained glass factory. The factory has been renovated in recent years as offices.*

106. *(Top left) The Bedfordbury Mission House, 1861. The architect was Arthur Blomfield.*

107. *(Bottom left) To cater for the large number of Irish in the Covent Garden area the Corpus Christi church in Maiden Lane was built in 1874. The architect was Frederick Pownall.*

108. *(Top right) The rectory of St Paul's church, Burleigh Street. It was built in 1860 as the rectory of St Michael's church, opposite it in the same street; the architect was William Butterfield. The church was opened in 1833 but, because of the dwindling population in the area, it closed in 1905. Part of the Strand Palace Hotel now stands on its site.*

Giles Christian Mission had a home for destitute women in Drury Lane, where there was also a Working Girls' Club. The same organisation also had a boys' home in Wild Street. In Shelton Street there was an Artisans' Institute for Promoting General and Technical Education and the Hanover House Home for Working Boys in London.

On the site of the Sanctuary in Floral Street was, in 1751, a school for poor children; this was superseded by the Adelphi School, so built that no noise could penetrate to King Street using the simple expedient of having no windows at its rear and side. The children were not allowed to play in the back courtyard. On one side was a brothel, which was replaced by a cowhouse. By the 1860s it was called Covent Garden Market School and from 1900 used as a club (religiously guided) for market workers.

109. The main entrance of the original buildings of Charing Cross Hospital.

CHARING CROSS HOSPITAL

Charing Cross Hospital is now in Fulham Palace Road, but it originated in 1818 in a small hospital established by Benjamin Golding. Golding, living just off Leicester Square, had been a student at St Thomas' Hospital. He was so distressed at the number of people needing medical attention, but unable to obtain it, that, as he wrote later, 'I opened my house in the year 1815 to such poor persons as desired gratuitous advice and presented myself daily for all such applicants from eight o'clock in the morning until one in the afternoon; and this practice I continued for several years.' This developed three years later into a hospital in Suffolk Street at the rear of the Haymarket Theatre called the West London Infirmary and Dispensary. Eight years later it was to be found in Villiers Street, south of the Strand, with room for twelve beds. Golding then planned what was to be a very large hospital indeed across the road on a site bounded now by Chandos Place and Agar Street, with the warm support of the Duke of Sussex. The Charing Cross Hospital, as it was then called, was opened in 1834 in a building designed by Decimus Burton. This was then gradually enlarged and included a medical school whose roll of pupils boasts David Livingstone, T.H. Huxley and the former Labour politician, Edith Summerskill.

The early staff of the hospital included a resident housekeeper or matron, a beadle, porter and other male servants. Coal was used for heating the wards, but all fires were put out at seven in the evening; there was to be no loud conversation and certainly no swearing; morning prayers were to be said by everyone in 'an audible voice'.

When the hospital moved to Fulham in 1973 the old building lay empty until determined work by the Greater London Council, particularly by Cllr Luke O'Connor, led to it being used for hostel accommodation for the homeless. This was later closed and the building has recently been converted to become new quarters for the Metropolitan Police.

110. Decimus Burton, architect of the Charing Cross Hospital.

Illustrious People

Famous residents of Covent Garden are mainly of the seventeenth to early nineteenth centuries. Once the market became overwhelming and the slum areas of Seven Dials and Drury Lane encroached, only the most impecunious would have moved into the area, though many no doubt used its taverns.

The landscape artist J.M.W. Turner (1775-1851) was born in Maiden Lane, on the south side on the site of No. 21. His father, a hairdresser, subsequently lived at No. 26, a house that the artist stayed at, from about 1790 to 1799, in apartments described by Joseph Farington as 'small and ill calculated for a painter'. Part of No. 26 consisted of auction rooms which were used by the Society of Artists of Great Britain. No. 21 has unaccountably been derelict for very many years and the site today is occupied by a grossly ugly mobile restaurant.

In the same street Andrew Marvell (1621-78) was in a house on the site of No. 9 in 1677, and Voltaire (1694-1778) was here, probably on the south side at the sign of the White Peruke, in 1727-8. Marvell at that time was Member of Parliament for Hull and had been a keen opponent of the Royalist party. It is recorded that while here he received a visit from an emissary of Charles II, who offered him some money to alleviate his poverty. Assuming the offer to be a bribe, Marvell refused and carried on dining from the remains of a mutton bone. He died the following year.

Thomas Arne (1710-78), whose musical career is today overshadowed by his composition of *Rule Britannia*, reverted to subterfuge as a boy to pursue his musical studies. His father, an upholsterer in King Street (the sign of the Crown and Cushion), disapproved of them and Arne secretly took violin lessons outside the house and played the spinet in his room at home, the strings of which he muffled with cloths. It was only when Arne was advanced enough to lead a string band that his father discovered what had been going on, but he was eventually persuaded to let talent ride its course. Arne was born in a house on the site of No. 31 and was buried in the churchyard of St Paul's across the road.

In Rose Street, then one of the worst addresses in Covent Garden, the wretchedly poor Samuel Butler (1612-80), author of *Hudibras*, lived. Here he died of consumption, but so few friends and supporters had he that a proposal to bury him in Westminster Abbey failed to find a seconder and he, like Arne, was to be interred in St Paul's Covent Garden.

111. J.M.W. Turner, by George Dance, 1800.

112. Andrew Marvell.

113. *Nos 26/7 Maiden Lane, the home of the Turner family.*

114. *Voltaire in 1732, after a portrait by la Tour.*

115. *Jane Austen, a drawing by her sister, Cassandra.*

Edmund Curll (1675-1747), publisher and bookseller, came to the authorities' notice, not for the first time, with a book, judged pornographic, entitled *A Treatise on the use of Flogging in Venereal Affairs*. Later, he lived and did business from Bow Street, next to Will's coffee-house; in 1733 he was to be found in Burleigh Street and in 1735, Rose Street. He died two years after publishing *The Pleasures of Coition*.

Notable residents of the Piazza have included Sir Henry Vane the Younger and Sir Kenelm Digby author and naval commander, who lived in the Piazza house before its rebuilding as No. 43 King Street. In the Great Piazza (the houses on the northern and north-eastern sides of the square), there was the surgeon William Hunter (No. 1, 1749-60), Thomas Killigrew, dramatist (No. 8, 1636-40 and 1661-2), painter Sir James Thornhill (No. 12, 1722-34), John Rich, theatre owner and impresario (No. 15, 1743-60), and Sir Godfrey Kneller, painter (Nos. 16-17, 1682-c1702).

The sculptor, John Flaxman (1755-1826), lived in New Row at his father's plaster shop (at the sign of the Golden Head), and it was from here that he sent his first contribution – a modelled head – to the Royal Academy.

A plaque off Bow Street records the residences of various notable men. The Fieldings, of course, were at the magistrate's court (see p72); Robert Harley, later to be the first 1st Earl of Oxford, was born here

in 1661 – his collection of books and manuscripts was to be one of the bases of the British Museum. Fellow bibliophile, Dr John Radcliffe (1650-1714), whose patients included William III and Queen Anne, left a sum of money which helped to found the Radcliffe Infirmary in Oxford. He lived in Bow Street from about 1684 and amassed a large fortune, especially after inheriting the clients of a physician in King Street who had died. Radcliffe's apothecary, who himself was worth £50,000 when he died, claimed that within a year of being in Bow Street, Radcliffe was earning twenty guineas a day. Many people, it is said, feigned illness so as to sample his conversation.

At No. 10 Henrietta Street there was from 1807-16 a bank called Austen, Maunde and Tilson. The 'Austen' was Jane Austen's brother, and on her visits to London in 1813 and 1814, she stayed above the business. When Dr Johnson first arrived in London from Lichfield he took lodgings in Exeter Street at the house of Richard Norris, a staymaker. The site of the house is now covered by Wellington Street.

Johnson's former pupil and later friend, the actor David Garrick (1717-79), had an extraordinary career in Covent Garden. He made a famous appearance as Richard III at the Goodman's Fields theatre in the East End in 1741, to which the fashionable of the West End flocked, no doubt in some confusion as to where the area was and relying heavily on their coachmen to

116. *Samuel Butler, from a drawing by T. Uwins.*

117. *John Flaxman.*

find it. Inevitably, he was lured to the Theatre Royal, Drury Lane, where he was highly successful. It was in Garrick's house in King Street that actors at the Theatre Royal gathered to decide what to do about the bankruptcy of the theatre's owner, since they were all owed money; from this meeting developed a serious quarrel with his old friend, Charles Macklin, the actor. In 1746 Garrick switched to performing at Covent Garden Theatre, then under the ownership of John Rich, but at the same time he took on part of the financial responsibility of the Theatre Royal. Thereafter, he was mainly to be found at the latter theatre.

After his marriage in 1747 (which disappointed a number of other ladies) he and his wife moved to 27 Southampton Street – the house survives. A number of actors who had fallen out with Garrick decamped to Covent Garden and there was great rivalry between the two theatres and their respective casts. This culminated, to the delight of the public, in both theatres staging *Romeo and Juliet* at the same time in 1750.

When the delicate poet, Thomas de Quincey (1785-1859), came to settle in London for the second time in 1821, he was already an opium addict. It was a drug which excited much interest amongst London society, and in his lodgings at 36 Tavistock Street he

wrote, to much acclaim, *Confessions of an Opium Eater*.

Other notables in Covent Garden have included the American writer, Washington Irving (1783-1859), who lodged with a friend at 22 Henrietta Street in 1824, the librettist W.S. Gilbert (1836-1911), born at 17 Southampton Street, Charles Lamb (with his sister) lodged at 20/21 Russell Street from 1817-23 and enjoyed the bustle of the place, and *Punch* founder and social writer, Henry Mayhew (1812-87), lived and died at 8 Tavistock Street.

Residents of Great Queen Street have included Sir Thomas Fairfax, prominent Parliamentary general in the Civil War, who received a congratulatory visit of a delegation from the House of Lords in 1647. Sir Godfrey Kneller, court painter, moved to this street from the Piazza and was here in 1719 when he wrote a letter to Alexander Pope. The young Joshua Reynolds studied art on the south side of the street in a house belonging to the painter, Thomas Hudson.

The dramatist, Richard Brinsley Sheridan (1751-1816) resided in a house in Great Queen Street now covered by the Freemasons' Hall, a stretch of the road which also contained James Boswell, who wrote his life of Dr Johnson here; on the other side of the road, William Blake (1757-1827), the poet, lived for three years at No. 31. Other residents of the street have included Mrs ('Perdita') Robinson, society hostess and actress, and the artists, John Opie and Richard Wilson.

118. *David Garrick in the role of Tancred. 'Painted, Etch'd & Sold by Tho. Worlidge, at his House in the little Piazza Covent Garden.'*

119. *Thomas de Quincey, from a chalk drawing by J. Archer, 1855.*

121. *Sir Joshua Reynolds, from a self-portrait.*

120. *Nos 34-38 Tavistock Street in 1958. De Quincey had lived at No. 36.*

122. *A typical trader in a street adjoining the market – Goldsmid's at No. 10 Henrietta Street, in 1938.*

Trading Places

Covent Garden was dominated, of course, by market traders. In the nineteenth century individual vendors increasingly used wholesalers, instead of selling in the market themselves. T.J. Poupart became one of the largest of these – the family was established in the market by 1776. George Monro, another of the principal traders, began with a market gardener selling his father's produce in 1862 and, before the move to Nine Elms, the company had its headquarters at 43 King Street (see Illustration 123).

One of the best known shops in Covent Garden had and has nothing to do with fruit and vegetables – Moss Bros. – no-one ever says Moss Brothers. This famous firm of tailors began in 1860 when Moses Moses opened a shop at 25 Bedford Street. Round the corner, in 1881, in that bit of King Street that leads west to New Row, his two sons opened a similar establishment. In between, a lacemaker occupied the corner site.

The speciality of Moss Bros. – hiring out dress suits – began, according to the company, in 1897, when one of the sons, Alfred Moss (the name had been Anglicized by then), had a stockbroker friend called Charles Pond. In his heyday Pond was much in demand at weekend house parties and though still invited when he fell on hard times, he could not afford the clothes appropriate to the occasions. He persuaded Moss to lend him a tail suit, returned it, then borrowed it again a number of times. Moss eventually asked him for a fee for this service – 7/6d – and realised that this could develop into a lucrative business.

Moss Bros. are now no longer on their old site (Tesco are) and instead are across the road in King Street, but they are still renowned for this aspect of their business.

Another famous retailer began at 173 Drury Lane – Sainsbury. The first shop of what is now the largest grocers in the country was opened in 1869 by John Sainsbury and his wife in a house that had three floors and an attic. His wife was the daughter of a dairyman in Somers Town, and he already had much experience of helping at shops in street markets. Sainsbury's original ambition as the business prospered (it was mainly dairy goods) was to open enough branches for each of his sons to manage – he had six sons and six daughters – but by the time of his death he had far exceeded what must have seemed at the start a formidable ambition. It was a major business by then,

123. *No. 43 King Street c.1932, during conversion works for George Monro.*

124. *Langley Court , off Long Acre, in 1911, one of many small courts containing market traders.*

125. *The first Moss Bros. shop at 20 Bedford Street.*

renowned for its clean shops and modern approach to food storage. It is said that Sainsbury's last words before he died in 1928 were "Keep the shops well lit".

Samuel French, the well-known publisher of plays, began in 1830 when 20-year-old Thomas Lacy set up shop in Wellington Street selling acting editions of plays. This just preceded the lifting of the monopoly of the Covent Garden and Drury Lane theatres, and the spur that this gave to new drama and new theatres galvanised the business. At about the same time Samuel French had begun a similar business in America and he exchanged scripts with Lacy. In 1878 French came to England, bought out Lacy, and developed the business until his death twenty years later.

At Nos. 27-8 King Street (where Moss Bros are now located) the Prince of Wales' emblem and the words WESTMINSTER FIRE OFFICE are emblazoned on an upper storey. Numerous fire insurance companies began in the eighteenth century. Most had their own brigade, which attended any fire involving premises the company insured – in 1833 the insurance brigades were merged to form a metropolitan fire brigade. The Westminster, one of the better known fire insurance companies in London, was formed in 1717, in Bedford Street by 1751, and in King Street from 1808. It was at this time that substantial alterations were made to the premises. The company is now a subsidiary of Alliance Assurance.

Next door, going west, were the auctioneers Debenham Storr, whose building was reconstructed in 1860 at the time of the formation of Garrick Street. Another auctioneer in the area was Sotheby's. This company began at what is now the junction of Tavistock Street and Wellington Street with a bookselling business, founded in 1744 by Samuel Baker. Ten years later he established the first saleroom to deal only with books, manuscripts and prints. In 1776, some years after his death, the business passed to his nephew, John Sotheby. The firm moved to 13 Wellington Street in 1817 and nearly one hundred years later to New Bond Street.

At the junction of Bedford Street and the Strand stood the large Civil Service Stores, virtually destroyed by fire in 1982, although much of the old exterior was rescued. The shop's odd name derived from an era of co-operative experiments, though these had been essentially working-class ventures so as to obtain cheaper food, with any profits being passed on to customers. The Civil Service Supply Association, as it came to be called, was begun in 1864 by clerks in the Post Office buying tea in bulk and selling in small quantities to those who had subscribed to the purchase. The scheme was extended to other foodstuffs and was sufficiently successful for it to be opened up to other civil servants and to allow the erection of a store on the Strand in 1870 which sold most of the items that families would normally require. The idea

126. *The first Sainsbury shop at 173 Drury Lane.*

127. *A saddler's at 138 Long Acre in 1903, a reminder of the street's former speciality of manufacturing coaches.*

128. *The Civil Service Stores in Bedford Street in 1877. The architects were Lockwood and Mawson.*

was copied by the Army and Navy Stores a year later.

Stanford's, the map and travel guide sellers in Long Acre, were established in Long Acre in the 1880s; their present building, designed by Herbert Read and Macdonald, was built in c1901.

129. *The former building of the Westminster Fire Office at Nos 27/8 King Street in 1967.*

130. *The former building of auctioneers Debenham Storr at the corner of King and Garrick Streets in 1968.*

131. *A book auction in progress at Sotheby's, Tavistock Street, in 1888.*

The New Theatres

THE THEATRE ROYAL

The era of David Garrick at the Theatre Royal, Drury Lane, from his acting debut there in 1742 until his retirement from its management in 1776, was one of the most notable in the history of what is London's longest surviving theatre. But even as he retired new idols were being fashioned. Richard Brinsley Sheridan took over the management of the theatre where his *School for Scandal* received its first performance in 1777. Sarah Siddons, who had had an inauspicious debut at the Theatre Royal during Garrick's reign, returned there in 1782 and became a sensation. The following year, her brother, John Philip Kemble joined

132. The pear-shaped Augustus Harris, who revived both the Theatre Royal and Covent Garden Theatre; cartoon by 'Spy'.

133. Edmund Kean – a sensational debut in 1814.

the cast and in 1788 became manager, though the capricious Sheridan was still owner. Kemble was to despair of Sheridan as much as had his predecessors and in 1803 he bought a third share of the Covent Garden patent and, with his sister, defected to Bow Street.

Acting styles were increasingly melodramatic and declamatory. In part this may have been a reaction of necessity to the larger auditoriums that then existed, but it is likely too that Londoners had a taste for their Shakespeare as dramatic as could be squeezed out of the text.

As we have seen (p31) the theatre that Garrick first knew was replaced in 1794, and that replacement was burned down in 1809. Once Sheridan had been eased out of affairs, a new building – substantially the one we see today – was erected by Benjamin Wyatt (the portico was added in 1820, the colonnade in 1831 and the auditorium refashioned in Empire style in 1922). This fourth Theatre Royal opened in October 1812, with a prologue written by Byron and a production of *Hamlet*.

The theatre was in the financial doldrums almost immediately, but it was rescued in January 1814 by the sensational debut of Edmund Kean. Coleridge said that Kean's acting was 'like reading Shakespeare by lightning flashes', but melodramatic or not, Kean carved out a relationship with his audiences that had

134. *John Philip Kemble, by Sir Thomas Lawrence.*

been rarely equalled, even by Garrick. His gaunt, prominent-eyed appearance brought realism to the tragic parts he played, and swift changes of moods encouraged the illusion of madness. Kean burnt himself out quickly. A frenzied private life, punctuated by an excess of drink and affairs, brought about a swift decline in his acting abilities. He died in 1833 at the age of 46.

The actor, William Macready, took over the Theatre Royal in 1841 and gradually improved the physical condition of the theatre, but it was still a financial millstone – Macready left after two years having lost about £20,000.

It was only in the 1870s that the Theatre Royal recovered its prestige under the management of Augustus Harris. Spectacular shows were produced – the equivalent of today's musicals – with elaborate scenic effects. Pantomime came each Christmas, melodrama reigned and music hall was often presented.

During the First World War the theatre became briefly a cinema, with presentations of the famous films made by D.W. Griffiths, *The Birth of a Nation* and *Intolerance*.

The years between the wars saw a greater emphasis on musicals. *The Desert Song* (1927), *Show Boat* (1928) and *New Moon* (1929) were all American imports, a foretaste of things to come. In 1931 Noel Coward's *Cavalcade* was produced and ran for 405 performances, and from 1935 light romantic musicals by Ivor Novello held sway – *Glamorous Night* (1935), *Careless Rapture* (1936), *Crest of the Wave* (1937) and *The Dancing Years* (1939).

During the Second World War the Theatre Royal became the headquarters of ENSA (the organisation that provided entertainment to the armed forces). Afterwards it reverted to American musicals – *Oklahoma!* (1947), *Carousel* (1950), *South Pacific* (1951), *The King and I* (1953), *My Fair Lady* (its opening scenes appropriately set in the Piazza, in 1958). More recently there has been *Billy*, *Chorus Line* and *Miss Saigon*.

THE OPERA HOUSE

The present building of the Royal Opera House was opened in May 1858, designed by E.M. Barry. The extension to the rear, which backs onto James Street, was erected in the 1980s and there are plans for further expansion now that a very large sum of lottery money has been made available. The first production was a shambles on opening night. The offering was the very long opera, *Les Huguenots*, which by half past midnight had still not reached its last act. A management decision to end it there was met by a hail of catcalls which not even the playing of the national anthem could subdue. Standards were not high, in

135. *The Floral Hall and Covent Garden Theatre in Bow Street.*

the 1870s and 1880s especially. George Bernard Shaw
noted that most of the Don Giovannis 'swaggered
through the part like emancipated billiard-markers'.
Wagner was accepted reluctantly. The first production at Covent Garden of *Lohengrin* was performed in
Italian (as the only respectable operatic language),
and went on until 12.50am, the conductor having
granted encores to the preludes of two Acts and one
scene. The insistence on Italian continued in Bow
Street long after the Theatre Royal and Her Majesty's
Theatre in the Haymarket were commonly using
German and French.

In 1888 Augustus Harris took over management
when the theatre was at its lowest ebb – thus both the
two theatres were again for a period under the same
administration. He revived Covent Garden and gave
it status and style again. In 1892 Harris imported a
German company to perform *The Ring*, with the young
Gustav Mahler as conductor. But Shaw still had little
of praise to describe performances: '.... for want of a
stage manager, no man in *Les Huguenots* knows

*136. Augustus Harris, with play characters; drawing by
Aubrey Beardsley, 1894.*

137. The Duchess Theatre.

whether he is a Catholic or a Protestant; and conversations which are pure nonsense except on the supposition that the parties cannot distinguish one another's features in the gloom are conducted in broad moonlight and gaslight.'

Before the First World War (during which the theatre became a furniture store) Diaghilev's Russian ballet was presented for several years, with Nijinksy and Karsavina as the premier dancers. The impact of these productions on ballet appreciation in this country cannot be overstated.

Sir Thomas Beecham brought opera back to Covent Garden after the First World War, but in 1920 Beecham was declared bankrupt and his opera company was dissolved. The Carl Rosa Company temporarily filled the void, yet so poor were the fortunes of the theatre that boxing matches and film shows were held there. But opera, especially German opera, picked up again and was going strong when war intervened again in 1939.

Covent Garden was a dance hall during the Second World War, but in 1944 it was taken by the music publishers, Boosey & Hawkes, to restore it to operatic use. After the war the first governmental support, via the forerunner of the Arts Council, was received. On 20 February 1946 the Royal Opera House was re-opened with a production of Tchaikovsky's ballet, *Sleeping Beauty*, danced by Margot Fonteyn and Robert Helpmann, with design by Oliver Messel.

The Carl Rosa Company and the Sadlers Wells Opera formed the basis of the Royal Opera and Sadler's Wells Ballet provided the Royal Ballet.

Productions since then have been ever more extravagant. The aim to establish the Royal Opera House as one of the leading three or four in the world, has inevitably meant competing with theatres abroad that are better funded. The rise in ticket prices to meet the shortfall and to allow the hiring of the best of singing talent, has encouraged a conviction that admission to the theatre is for the affluent only – hence genuine indignation in 1995 when the Opera House was granted a seemingly disproportionate amount of Lottery money for expansion and improvement.

ADDITIONS AND SUBTRACTIONS

The Lyceum (see p35) was rebuilt as a vast music-hall in 1904, designed by Bertie Crewe to rival the Coliseum in St Martin's Lane (the portico of the old theatre was retained). It was a financial disaster and the theatre closed in six months, though the Coliseum, initially a success, also had serious problems soon afterwards.

Popular drama was presented successfully there from 1907 until 1939, when John Gielgud's *Hamlet* was the last production. Demolition was announced that year and redevelopment planned, but the Lon-

138. *The Novelty (or Kingsway) Theatre in Great Queen Street, 1904.*

don County Council refused permission because it too had plans for the site, and then war intervened and the theatre was left empty. The LCC's plans had changed when the war ended and the Lyceum was let as a dance hall instead. It is now empty and awaiting its fate.

The Middlesex Music Hall in Drury Lane opened in 1911, the successor to several smaller ventures attached to public houses. Designed by Frank Matcham, it was one of the largest theatres in London, but its fortunes were mixed. It became the Winter Gardens Theatre in 1919, but with theatre audiences leaving music hall behind them and drifting westwards to the sophistications of Shaftesbury Avenue and Charing Cross Road, it was sold after the last war by its owners, Rank Organisation, to a property company that was permitted to demolish it. However, they were obliged to reinstate a theatre within the office complex that was built, and this is the present New London Theatre, designed by Sean Kenny and opened in 1973. This has been the home of the musical *Cats* for as long as most teenagers can remember.

The Duchess Theatre in Catherine Street (Illustration 137) was opened in 1929. The design by Ewen Barr is ingenious, since the building had to comply with a number of regulations and ancient lights requirements. It is, however, a modest building, unsuited to much advertising on its fascia and has a

139. St Martin's Music Hall, Long Acre in 1853.

140. The Queen's Theatre, successor to St Martin's Music Hall, in 1867.

141. *Evans' Music Hall, built in the rear yard of No. 43 King Street.*

142. *Ellen Terry.*

of an old tavern, and includes within it a passageway to the side which leads to the Scottish National Church in Crown Court at the rear. Designed by Ernest Schaufelberg, it is a good looking building and one of the few theatres built in London during this architectural period. Its most famous productions have been *At the Drop of a Hat* with Michael Flanders and Donald Swann (1957), and *Beyond the Fringe* (1961), which introduced Peter Cook, Dudley Moore, Alan Bennett and Jonathan Miller to London audiences.

Two theatres have disappeared altogether. One went under a large number of names in increasingly unavailing attempts to gain audiences, but was usually called the Novelty or Kingsway Theatre. It was in Great Queen Street, by Newton Street, and opened in 1882, with reconstruction in 1900. It saw the first English productions of Ibsen's *The Doll's House* (1889), and Synge's *Playboy of the Western World* (1907). The theatre was bombed in 1941 and did not reopen afterwards.

On the north side of Long Acre, the Queen's Theatre was opened in 1867, paid for by the owner of the *Daily Telegraph*. With a seating capacity of 4,000, it was then one of the largest theatres in London and in its prime was home to Irving and Ellen Terry. But it was a short-lived venture and closed in 1878, whereupon it became a co-operative store, a gymnasium for the Young Men's Christian Association, offices and warehouse premises, and eventually one of the buildings used by the printers, Odhams. The Queen's was on the site of the St Martin's Music Hall, opened in 1850 for a Mr John Hullah, at which Dickens sometimes gave readings.

The Players' Theatre, which began in 1927 in New Compton Street, began the London career of Peggy Ashcroft. In 1934 it moved to the top floor of 43 King Street, a house which had once contained Evans' Music Hall in its rear basement, and in 1937 it produced its first Victorian music hall: this form of entertainment was to be the staple fare of the Players' Theatre in more recent years. By 1946 the company was in Villiers Street, beneath the arches of the Charing Cross railway station.

Since the departure of the Covent Garden Market fringe theatre has appeared in a number of the old warehouses in the surrounding streets. Of particular quality and interest have been productions at the Donmar Warehouse in Earlham Street.

small auditorium. Despite this, its production history includes some interesting plays. There were three new plays by J.B. Priestley in the 1930s and, in 1935, the first production of Emlyn Williams' *Night Must Fall*. *Murder in the Cathedral* by T.S. Eliot had its first London production here in 1936 and when war intervened another Williams play, *The Corn is Green*, was playing to packed audiences. After the war Coward's *Blithe Spirit* ran for nearly 2,000 performances, and Pinter's *The Caretaker* transferred here from the Arts Theatre in 1960 and ran for a year.

The Fortune Theatre in Russell Street also has a small auditorium. This was opened in 1924 on the site

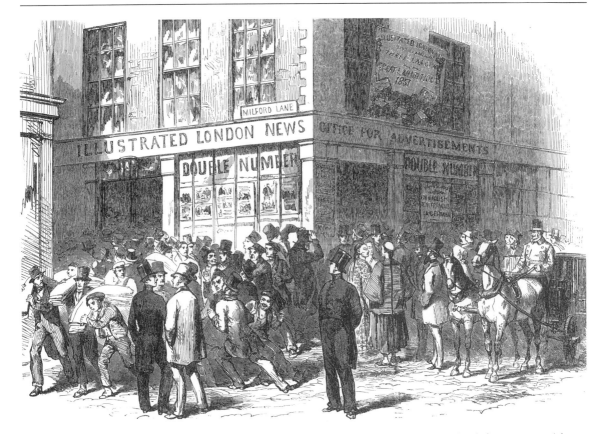

143. A gathering of potential readers outside the offices of The Illustrated London News *in 1851, just before a new, special, edition was due to appear.*

The Fourth Estate

POPULAR TASTES

From the mid-nineteenth century the growth of newspapers in Fleet Street was matched by a vast expansion of magazine publishing, much of it centred on the Strand and Covent Garden. This explosion of the printed word had its roots in the abolition of the Newspaper Stamp Duty in 1855, the growing numbers of people who were literate and the availability of railways to achieve national circulations.

The presence of so many publishers of magazines in Covent Garden most probably resulted from earlier convenience, when each journal had to be stamped at the Stamp Duty Office located at Somerset House. Illustration 144 shows copies of the most successful magazine of its period, *The Illustrated London News*, which was published in Milford Lane, just off the Strand, being loaded on to a cart for transportation to the Office, a tedious and time-consuming business. At its height, especially during the French Revolution

144. Delivery of copies of The Illustrated London News *to Somerset House for stamping, in 1852, three years before the Stamp Duty on newspapers was abolished.*

when the government had felt distinctly insecure, the Stamp Duty was prohibitive enough to place news and comment well out of the financial reach of those sections of the community the authorities thought most likely to be influenced by revolutionary ideas.

When the journalistic deluge eventually reached the common man the content was, to a great extent, educational rather than political.

Three Covent Garden publishers were prominent names in the mass market. George Newnes at Nos 8-14 Southampton Street was one of them. While working in a fancy goods store in Manchester, Newnes (1851-1910), conceived of the idea of a magazine full of interesting items of miscellaneous information. These he called 'tit-bits', and the magazine of that name he launched in 1881 on the streets of Manchester sold 5,000 copies in two hours. It was to be the base of his fortune. He moved to London and soon had premises in Burleigh Street and Southampton Street; he increased the circulation of his extraordinary magazine by giving away houses, or insurance against railway accidents. One of his prizes, a job in the *Tit-bits* office, was won by a young man called Cyril Arthur Pearson who, as we shall see, was to become a major rival. Another member of the staff was Alfred Harmsworth, who answered questions from correspondents: Harmsworth, later to be Lord Northcliffe, left Newnes to set up his own miscellaneous information magazine called *Answers*. Newnes went on to publish the highly successful *Strand* magazine, a form of illustrated popular literature. In 1893 he began the *Westminster Gazette*, a liberal paper. Other titles in Southampton Street included *Wide World Magazine*, *Woman's Life* and *Woman at Home*. More lastingly, he helped to found *Country Life* in 1897 in association with an eccentric and rich printer, Edward Hudson, well-known for his habit of crossing the Strand each day to lunch while imperiously holding up his hand to halt the traffic.

The young and scarcely educated Pearson, noted above, won his prize of a clerkship at Newnes when he was only eighteen and did well – he was appointed manager a year later, although his salary never exceeded £350. In 1890 he left to pursue his own fortune and published *Pearson's Weekly*, a magazine of light fiction, competitions and information. Other publications of his were *Home Notes* and *Short Stories*. In 1900 he was rich enough from the *Weekly* to begin the *Daily Express*, a newspaper selling at the then lowest price of a halfpenny, four years after Harmsworth had launched the *Daily Mail*.

But disaster struck in 1908 when he was virtually blinded by glaucoma and after having disposed of three of his newspapers, including the *Evening Standard*, he devoted the rest of his life to the problems of blind people – he became totally blind himself in a few years.

145. *The Catherine Street headquarters of The Builder, one of the most influential magazines of the second half of the nineteenth century.*

Pearson came to national attention during the First World War when the number of blinded soldiers was a serious problem for the authorities. He opened a hostel for them in the Bayswater Road and then transferred it to a house called St Dunstan's in Regent's Park, from which his organisation eventually took its name. He died tragically in 1921 after slipping in his bath and drowning.

The third of this trio of disseminators of popular magazines was Julius Elias, whose career with Odhams Press is described on pp56-9.

Most enduring in Covent Garden has been *The*

146. *The Burleigh Street offices of* Tit-bits.

Lady, a magazine whose content and layout seems an anachronism in modern publishing. It was launched in 1885 by Thomas Gibson Bowles, already the publisher and editor of *Vanity Fair*, which he had founded at the age of 26 in 1868. The two magazines, one for middle to upper-class ladies, and the other a satirical/society paper, were published from Tavistock Street.

The Lady was not the first women's paper, though the market at that time was undeveloped. C.L. Dodgson (Lewis Carroll) objected to the wording of one of its advertisements which proclaimed that 'To look beautiful is one of the first duties of a lady.' The first edition sold 2361 copies and lost £209. The two magazines moved to 39/40 Bedford Street in 1881, where printing presses were installed in the basement, and there *The Lady* has remained since. One of its most famous members of staff, even if of brief duration, was Stella Gibbons, the future author of *Cold Comfort Farm*.

For long located in Covent Garden was *The Stage* weekly newspaper, bible of the acting profession: this was in Tavistock Street for many years, but is now in Bermondsey. *The Builder* was at 4 Catherine Street in a building specially designed for it. This publication was one of the most influential of the nineteenth century, its editor, George Godwin, promoting good architectural style and social reform in equal measure, with the aid of wonderful engravings.

There were some newspapers away from the purlieus of Fleet Street. The *News of the World* was printed in Exeter Street for twenty years, and on the site of Nos. 25-31 Wellington Street a now largely forgotten newspaper, *Reynold's News*, was founded in the mid-nineteenth century. It was the personal publication of George MacArthur Reynolds (1814-79), who in 1848 had chaired a noisy meeting of Chartists in Trafalgar Square, and was subsequently carried triumphantly to his house in Wellington Street; he also presided at the famous Chartist demonstration that year at Kennington Common. This radical politician began *Reynold's Weekly News* in 1850 which, in the words of the *Dictionary of National Biography*, became the mouthpiece of 'republican and advanced working class opinion'. It was also powerful ammunition in the hands of those who did not want to abolish the Stamp Duty on newspapers, for if such publications should abound.....! As it was the railway companies refused to have it sold on their platforms because it encouraged trade unionism. In its later years the paper was adopted by the Co-operative movement, but at the end in the 1970s, when its circulation was failing badly, its name was changed to *The Sunday Citizen*, which is enough (and was) to kill off any publication.

BOOKMEN

The major publishers were to be found in Bloomsbury and Covent Garden from the nineteenth century until recent years. No doubt, the relaxed atmosphere of Covent Garden, encouraged by the market and the theatres, was an attraction, and the rents were probably low in Henrietta and Bedford Streets because of their closeness to the congestion. Old street directories are rife with names now gone altogether, or else they are just imprints of much larger concerns. Other names have in themselves become large conglomerates. Alexander Macmillan, co-founder of the company of that name, brought the business to No. 16 Bedford Street and in 1872 moved it to Nos 29-30. Macmillans were already a success, for they had first published Kingsley's *Westward Ho!* and, in 1857, *Tom Brown's Schooldays*.

William Heinemann (1863-1920) began his own business in 1890. He launched a whole series of now-

147. The offices of Frederick Warne & Co at 14-16 Bedford Street, at which Beatrix Potter would have delivered her earlier manuscripts.

famous names – Stevenson, Galsworthy, Wells, Masefield, Beerbohm, Conrad, Lawrence, Maugham etc. and was, it was generally agreed, the best and most influential fiction publisher of his time. His offices were at Nos 20-21 Bedford Street.

Frederick Warne founded his own business at No. 15 Bedford Street in 1865 after several years association with his brother-in-law, George Routledge, another publisher. Warne initiated a famous series, the Chandos Classics, consisting of 154 volumes, which sold five million copies. He published *Nuttall's Dictionary*, once a well-known publication, and went on to children's books by Randolph Caldecott and Kate Greenaway. The firm's most successful books, published after Warne's death, were those of Beatrix Potter. Warne's published twenty-four of her timeless books during a relationship that stretched over thirty-three years from the time that Potter was a severely parented young woman to her later years when she was remarkably rich and independent on royalties. It was only at the age of thirty-nine that Beatrix Potter had sufficient courage to become engaged to Norman Warne, son of Frederick, but he died a few months later.

Another man who launched a million books from Bedford Street was Joseph Malaby Dent (1849-1926), whose premises, specially built for the firm, still survive at Nos 10-13 Bedford Street. Dent was a bookbinder by profession and had a bindery in Hoxton. He dabbled in publishing as from 1888, when he issued two books in what became the familiar 'Temple' series, and he continued to publish the classics in small, well-printed but cheap editions. But in 1904 a far more ambitious project developed – the Everyman Library. The plan was to produce 1,000 of the world's greatest books, and in the first twelve months 153 volumes were issued, an astounding turnover produced, as is normal in book publishing, by a small and underpaid staff.   Of Dent, Frank Swinnerton (who worked for him) said: 'Dent was lame, rather under middle height, hobbled very thoughtfully, looked over his spectacles as well as through them, sometimes relapsed into a Yorkshire phrase and accent, and was so silvery that many strangers mistook him for a saint. He had an unusually violent temper, which led him to scream alarmingly at members of his staff and address them, his head thrown back and his beard waggling, as "You donkey!" He never praised; he paid very poorly; he frightened everybody who worked for him; and he one day said wistfully to me, "I don't know how it is; but when we get anybody who is any good he always leaves us."'

Another forceful personality, given to extremes, was Victor Gollancz (1893-1967), who founded his own firm at 14 Henrietta Street in 1928. His first success soon afterwards was the play, *Journey's End*,

by R.C. Sherriff, and he also published Daphne du Maurier and Dorothy L. Sayers. With the distinctive typography and yellow colour of his jackets, devised by Stanley Morison, Gollancz made a speciality of crime stories. In 1936 he founded the Left Book Club, a series of volumes which promoted the Left and warned against Fascism.

Also in Henrietta Street were Duckworth's at Nos 3-4 from the turn of the century to the 1950s, followed by newcomers MacGibbon and Kee, and at Nos 7-8 were Ballière Tindall, medical publishers. The novelist, Gillian Tindall, daughter of one of the partners, remembers talk of a ghost on the premises.

148. *The splendid new offices of publishers, Curtice & Co. in Catherine Street, erected in 1877.*

Lesser Places

The piecemeal and unstructured development of the Bedford estate outside of the wall erected in 1613 (see p9), and the haphazard spread of roads in the surrounding areas, resulted in numerous courtyards being formed, most of which quickly became the insanitary refuge of the poor. In particular, Drury Lane had courtyards east and west, many of which have been erased by the erection of Peabody Buildings or road improvements. But several remain, sanitised and rebuilt for the most part, reminders of the complex and quite unplanned jumbles of courts and alleys which festered in many areas of London. In the eighteenth century no less than 27 such unlit, unhygienic courts led off either side of Drury Lane between Long Acre and the Strand, some of them interconnecting and enough to deter even the bravest Bow Street Runner. Broad Court, Martlett Court and Crown Court are relics of that intricate and intensive use of land.

149. The Scottish National Church in Crown Court, opened in 1719.

THE SCOTTISH NATIONAL CHURCH

Crown Court contains the Scottish National Church, which is approached through an entrance now tucked into the side of the Fortune Theatre in Russell Street. This Presbyterian church has been here since 1719, when its congregation made a move from a building off St Martin's Lane. It was officially 'the Kirk of the Crown of Scotland' and, most likely, the court got its present name from that old title. In 1884 such was the overcrowding on Sundays that a new building (St Columba's) was erected in Pont Street, Chelsea, which drew away the more fashionable and wealthy of the Crown Court congregation, leaving behind a small membership and a building very badly in need of repair. Almost certainly it was felt at the time that the Crown Court building had served its purpose and would soon be demolished.

But in 1905 the new minister at Crown Court enlisted the aid of Lady Frances Balfour, sister-in-law of the Prime Minister, in a bid to renovate or rebuild the older building. By then the numbers in the congregation had dwindled still further. But, as Lady Balfour noted, 'At the usual evening service, in particular, there is a most interesting gathering of young Scotsmen and Scotswomen, in the anxious beginnings of London careers and therefore as yet far from affluent,

150. *New Row in 1966. New Street, as it was first called, appears on the earliest maps of Covent Garden. Building commenced in 1635 and it was finished by 1644, replacing two small alleyways. The Countess of Chesterfield and, later, Lady Stanhope, lived in a house on the site of the White Swan, pictured above.*

ardently attached to the Church of their native land, and in circumstances particularly calling for its aid.'

After negotiations with the Bedford Estate it was decided to release part of the land the Church occupied and rebuild on a smaller site, with an entrance from Russell Street. The architect, Eustace Balfour, devised an unusual plan in which the ground floor of the building was taken up by a hall for educational and social uses, with the church above it. The new church opened in 1909.

Broad Court, to the north of Crown Court, was rebuilt almost entirely in 1897 by R.C. Wornum. The original turning, New Broad Court, housed a multitude of small businesses which included an umbrella maker, a theatrical costumier, a ladies' school and a hatter. Douglas Jerrold (1803-57), author of a highly successful play, *Black-eyed Susan*, lived here in 1816. He joined the Mulberry Club, a gathering of theatrical people, which met at the Wrekin Tavern in Broad Court.

SOUTH OF MAIDEN LANE

Three very narrow courts lead down from Maiden Lane to the Strand. One is Bull Inn Court – named after an inn facing the Strand. This alleyway now consists of the sides of buildings, but for all that has a prominent part in the history of famous murders. It was here in 1897, at the stage door of the Adelphi Theatre, that the actor, William Terriss, who had arrived to play a leading role in a play called *Secret Service*, was stabbed to death by a man called Richard Prince, who was insanely convinced that he and not Terris should be playing the part.

Exchange Court contains one of the handsomest houses in Covent Garden – Nos. 1-5. It was for many years the headquarters of the Corps of Commissionaires, the organisation that provides security guards of the older and more welcoming school. The Corps was founded in 1859 by Captain Sir Edward Walter as a way of providing employment for wounded or pensioned servicemen. The Court probably takes its name from being directly opposite the New Exchange, a commodity bourse built early in the seventeenth century on the site of Durham House on the Strand. Off Exchange Court is Heathcock Court.

151. Demolition at the junction of Chandos Street and Bedford Street. The Chandos Street area was 'improved' in the 1820s with the construction of William IV and Adelaide Streets. A large number of courtyards were erased at that time and others were taken down when Charing Cross Hospital was built.

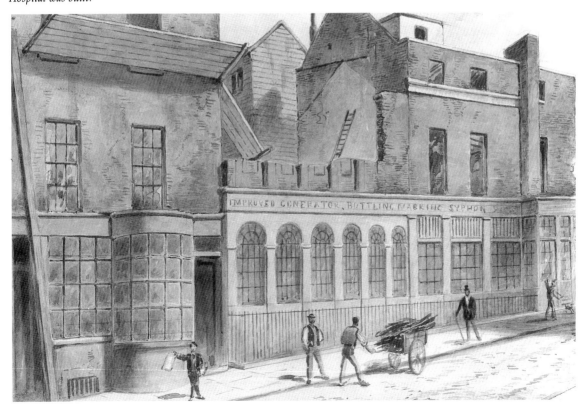

152. Exchange Court.

153. *Chandos Street in 1851.*

BEDFORDBURY

At one time seven courts ran between Bedfordbury and St Martin's Lane but now only Hop Gardens, May's Court, Goodwin's Court and the mysterious Brydges Place remain. Hop Gardens is named from a hop garden in the locality owned by Sir Hugh Platt in the early seventeenth century. May's Court is named after a builder who reconstructed it in 1739.

Goodwin's Court is a remarkable survivor. It consists of two rows of cottages, some with bow windows. A plaque on a wall claims that they were built c.1690, though Pevsner thinks they were late eighteenth century. Occupied mainly by tailors in the nineteenth century, they were condemned as residences in 1936 but allowed for office use.

NEAL'S YARD

An alley connecting Shorts Gardens and Monmouth Street widens out in its centre to form Neal's Yard, a place now with a high reputation for selling foodstuffs. Until recent years the warehouses here were bound up with the activities of the fruit and vegetable market – a large area used by a wheelwright, another was occupied by packing-case manufacturers, together with a potato salesman. In the 1970s it still contained a firm of armourers, called Robert White.

OFF LONG ACRE

Conduit Court probably takes its name not from a water supply, but from Leonard Cunditt, an inn holder in Long Acre c1686. Until demolition in 1954, it contained two bay-windowed shops, one of which was a cobbler's patronised by Sir Henry Irving.

Banbury Court is named after the Earl of Banbury who lived in Long Acre in the seventeenth century and Langley Court, like Langley Street opposite, was named for Sir Roger Langley of the Inner Temple, who held land in this area in the eighteenth century. Langley Court was called Blackamoor Alley in the seventeenth century, and by the time of Rocque's map of c.1746 was called Leg Alley, probably after the Golden Leg public house on the corner with Long Acre.

154. *Goodwin's Court, between Bedfordbury and St Martin's Lane, in the 1950s.*

155. *Neal's Yard, now home to organic foods and restaurants.*

156. *Brownlow House in Betterton Street. This road, between Endell Street and Drury Lane, still contains this fine eighteenth-century house, which derived its name from Sir James Brownlow, owner of Lennox House in Drury Lane (demolished c.1682). Dirty Lane, connecting the road to Long Acre, was virtually opposite.*

The road was originally called Brownlow Street, but changed to Betterton Street in 1877, in honour of the seventeenth-century Shakespearean actor, Thomas Betterton.

157. *Professional pea shellers at Covent Garden in the 1920s. They were employed to supply hotels and restaurants.*

A Market Place Abandoned

The removal of the market to the fringes of inner London had been a prospect for many years before it finally happened, but the difficulties of ownership and two world wars had delayed it. There were, of course, many who mourned its going. Despite its congestion, its disorganisation and its locational disadvantages, it had atmosphere and was truly a part of the nature of London – it is unlikely that many Londoners make a nocturnal trip to Nine Elms to savour sights and sounds there.

The market buildings were, however, only part of the story, for around them many of the premises were taken up by produce and ancillary firms whose rough usage of old warehouses and residences had reduced the overall fabric of the hinterland to a sorry state.

The Greater London Council published a Comprehensive Development Plan for the area in 1968 – about 100 acres were involved. It was envisaged that about 60% of the area was to be razed, approximately 2,000 people rehoused and many small businesses uprooted. A major road, parallel to the Strand, was planned, below surface level, on the line of Maiden Lane opening up a 'strong visual link with [the] Piazza' from the Strand, and another similar highway

at Shorts Gardens. Hotels and conference centres were to be built in this 'exceptional opportunity' for replanning a central part of London. There was to be a 'line of character' from Leicester Square to Lincoln's Inn Fields' which would contain buildings such as the main market, St Paul's church, the Opera House etc., worthy of conservation. It was suggested that the old Piazza might be reinvented, with arcaded buildings to the north and east.

The planners had learnt from the mistakes of a previous generation and recognised that the area contained a wide variety of close-knit trades – printing, theatrical and craft – and wanted to retain that commercial vibrancy. However, there was no recreational open space and therefore a 4-acre plot with a sports centre was proposed to straddle Long Acre – the very area in which the warehouses and factories containing many of these small companies were. There were also no car parks, other than those on bomb sites, and these would need to be built.

In the Plan published by the Council there are many descriptions of existing streets. In Neal Street for example, 'one finds a coppersmith who still makes and tins pots and pans in the traditional artisan's way, and directly behind this establishment there is a factory making precision engineering components. A bit further along the street is a Moslem grocer and two doors away, a maker of fretted musical instruments. Around the corner is a contract furniture

158. *A woman at Covent Garden market who made a modest living minding the whips of the carters who came to deliver goods.*

showroom, next door The Craft Centre, and beyond that one finds a rehearsal theatre and a fruit and vegetable warehouse.' And yet, despite the charm of the area that exudes from that description, the accompanying map places Neal Street in an area in urgent need of redevelopment.

What the scheme did not propose was an increase in offices, though it is fair to say that only half the existing office space was to be retained, leaving 1½ million sq. ft of offices to be rebuilt, much of it in high rise form. Residential space would be dramatically increased, shops would be doubled, hotels would be trebled and entertainment and the arts would be doubled. Car parking spaces would rise from zero to over 1½ million sq. ft. On the face of it these proposals could seem socially responsible, but to achieve them it meant that much of the existing hinterland around the Piazza would have to be demolished so that the land use could be intensified. No amount of 'lines of character' provision could change that fact.

It was an era of comprehensive planning and the conservation backlash was still gathering strength. It was not until 1971, when a Public Inquiry was begun into the scheme, that local residents became organ-ised to fight the proposals and they were aided by a recession in 1973 which made the building of new office blocks less attractive. By then there was also a noticeable trend in large companies to move their corporate headquarters out of central London into less expensive places such as Hammersmith.

By then too the accepted wisdom of handling traffic in towns, largely postulated by Dr Buchanan in his *Traffic in Towns*, was being questioned. In fact, it was heretically being asked if traffic should be allowed into towns at all, let alone encouraged into new arteries. In any case, grandiose plans for city centres were now the object of hostile suspicion. The experiences of many provincial towns and the awesome example of the Barbican were sufficient to produce not just 'sound-bite' reactions, but 'picture-bites'. The word 'concrete' was never far from 'jungle'. The public and the press had had enough of planners and no longer treated them with the respect the profession thought appropriate.

As it happens, planners are rarely correct in their predictions of what will happen in cities and by the time their plans come to fruition – if they do – the world has moved on and kicked away their assump-

159. *The legendary flower-sellers at Covent Garden, in the 1920s.*

160. One of the many market-related traders in Covent Garden – Ellen Keeley, barrow manufacturer, at 33 Neal Street in 1968.

tions. Yet, and this is the problem, though the market and some buildings were safe, what about the hinterland? How could it be left to the whims of market forces?

There were rumblings of second thoughts at the GLC and in Camden, two of the three partners in the scheme (Westminster was the third). In July 1972 Lady Dartmouth resigned as chair of the Covent Garden Committee, claiming that 'No individuals or bodies who represent the general public have supported us, and I have felt increasingly that our proposals are out of tune with public opinion which fears that the area will become a faceless, concrete jungle.'

The Secretary of State for the Environment was also discouraging. In his decision, announced in January 1973 (the year the market moved to Nine Elms), he endorsed the concept of a comprehensive plan, but rejected the intrusive road network and called for a new plan. More pertinently, he listed an additional 245 buildings in the area, thereby killing any prospect of comprehensive development. This bizarre judgement, a mixture of approval and prevention, was politically finely tuned, but there was no disguising the fact that the scheme was dead.

Meanwhile plans were made for the restoration of the main market building and controversy remained as to the future of the Jubilee Hall. Oddly, the GLC despite all appeals to the contrary, stuck to its intention to demolish the Jubilee Hall on the corner of the Piazza and Southampton Street. Here operated a flourishing market at street level and a community sports hall upstairs, the sort of commercial and community involvement that the now abandoned Plan seemed to support. It may be that the GLC had bought the Hall at a price which took into account profitable redevelopment, and it was not prepared to lose out. The Hall, a 1904 building, was eventually demolished and rebuilt, but not before important archaeological finds were made beneath (see p8).

The restoration of Fowler's market building is a showpiece renovation, though it was not achieved without some interesting arguments among conservationists. Purists wished to dispense with the roof, since it was not part of Fowler's original design, and the decision to dig down into the basement from the Central Avenue to form courtyards and provide an extra retail floor at basement level, also excited opposition. Some wanted to erect the colonnades up and down the Central Avenue that Fowler had envisaged but which were never built. These would, however, have not appealed to modern retailers whose shop windows would have been darkened, and would have severely limited the space for restaurants in the Avenue itself. More mundanely, as Robert Thorne points out in his excellent book on the restoration of the building, the change of use from market to retail shops brought the building within the clutches of various health and safety regulations that the market had managed to evade by virtue of its old charter. Therefore much expenditure was involved making good shortcomings with very little to show for it.

On the south-east corner of the Piazza the Plan's intention was to demolish the old Flower Market, but in 1973 it was one of those buildings which was additionally listed. The proposal to redevelop the site as a conference centre was therefore abandoned and further uses had to be considered. The London Transport Museum was chosen to occupy most of this building. This collection of vehicles had begun at the Chiswick works of the London General Omnibus Company in the 1920s. By 1973 it was housed at Syon Park and in 1980 it moved to Covent Garden.

The Theatre Museum, for long a part of the Victoria & Albert Museum collections in South Kensington, moved to the remainder of the Flower Market building in 1987. Here was brought together other material in private hands.

The Floral Hall's future has still to be determined. For years it had been in the occupation of its original owners – the Royal Opera House – used as a props' store. Plans in recent years to enlarge the theatre have entailed the demolition of the Floral Hall, but at the time of writing it is envisaged that some bays will be retained at the Bow Street end of the site.

161. *A typical unloading scene at the market in 1968.*

162. *The boarded-up market building in the late 1970s.*

163. *A daily scene in the restored market building.*

Present Pastures

There are no precedents in London's history for the rapid transformation of Covent Garden since the removal of the market. All predictions have been confounded and the influx of restaurants, studios, niche shops and above all, of tourists, is beyond any earlier London experience.

The abandonment by the Greater London Council of its grandiose redevelopment proposals, noted in the previous chapter, left a considerable if welcome vacuum. It left, in fact, more opportunities than there was imagination to satisfy for at no time previously have so many run-down premises, many of them suitable for retail trade, come on to the property market in such abundance. Nor have so many empty warehouses, some of great potential, been available in central London. This plenitude, however, prompted more questions than answers. If the central market building contained shops intended for tourists, what shops, what occupations should be in Long Acre, Neal Street and in the inner grid of roads? Who

indeed was to replace the market traders, and who pay for the renovation of their buildings? Should there be positive discrimination in favour of craft or 'community' businesses in the form of low rentals? Should there be an expansion of residential property and if so should it be low-rent or high-rent? How much office building should there be, and who should erect it?

The answers to such questions depended upon fundamental concepts. Many saw the area as predominantly residential, containing pockets of 'useful' household shops and workshops, with the Piazza and its showpiece market buildings stimulating the local economy. This approach was the antithesis of the way in which whole areas of London had previously been torn down, with communities of residents and businesses uprooted while redevelopment took place. Others wanted to see a considerable amount of arts activities concentrated in the area to complement the high profile organisations already functioning.

Others felt that the viable rejuvenation of the area depended upon commercial exploitation, but it was unclear what sort of businesses would take advan-

164. *The disappointing successor to the old Jubilee Hall, one of the few reminders of the GLC's development plan.*

tage of the premises available for even then, when the trend was to move large corporations out of central London, those remaining knew only the comforts and predictability of modern office blocks rather than the uncharted potential of warehouse conversions. However, not even those most enthusiastic for intervention of market forces could have foreseen just how intensely the whole of the area was to be affected by the commercial success of the central market building.

This metamorphosis has also been influenced by forces that planners could not have foreseen or withstood. Three notable trends stand out. One is the enormous increase in dining-out. This is not, of course, simply a Covent Garden phenomenon – even quite suburban areas such as Teddington have been affected by it. In the inner suburb of Islington, where fifteen years ago nightlife revolved quietly around two or three good restaurants and some public houses, a wide variety of ethnic restaurants and spruced-up pubs have more recently made for crowded pavements. In Soho, determined local residents have driven out much of the sleaze and restaurants have largely taken over.

The second trend is another which is common countrywide – the disappearance of small household

shops and the concentration of such shopping in large, sometimes out-of-town supermarkets. Despite the influx of affluent workers and tourists the remaining old-style shops in the area (and there weren't many anyway) have been driven out by reduced custom from local residents, lower margins and higher rents. The only department store in the area, the Civil Service Stores, was burnt down, together with its food hall, and was not superseded until quite recently when Tesco opened a Metro store on the old Moss Bros. site. Apart from this most retail premises have been taken by what are called niche shops which sell high mark-up merchandise of appeal to tourists or to those making special purchases.

The third trend was a surge of new, media-linked companies, who required premises where the limited square-footage they could afford was offset by unusual architecture or decor – the same amount of space in a conventional office block would be boring and without an appealing image. The Covent Garden warehouses were ideal for such conversions and small studios, advertising agents, typesetters and video and film companies found that the working spaces and the atmosphere of the area were right for their purposes.

165. *A very well restored building in Long Acre, now used as a clothes store.*

166 and 167. Exterior and interior views of a new shopping complex between Shorts Gardens and Earlham Street.

168. The celebrated clock in Shorts Gardens, near the entrance to Neal's Yard.

By the end of the 1980s Covent Garden market and its hinterland summed up the new media word – 'Style'. This linguistic umbrella sheltered anything from organic foods in Neal's Yard, fashion off Long Acre, dance studios in Floral Street and Langley Street, eating out (but not in the market building itself, which was strictly for the tourists), rap dancing in front of St Paul's, wine bars and specialist shops.

In this way Covent Garden has become a metropolitan spectacle, largely given over to tourists, to young people in particular, and to affluence, to shops selling items that are rarely needed and to businesses that operate within an unreal but profitable media world. The residential life that goes on around all this, much of it in the unlovely blocks built by nineteenth-century charities, is unnoticed and unconsidered. These residents are remote from the new nature of Covent Garden and whatever connections with the old market building that existed before, perhaps of occasional work, or even just of working-class camaraderie, have disappeared.

Ironically, Covent Garden now fulfills many of the discarded intentions of the planners, but without the disadvantages they had in mind of concrete, new roads, hotels and convention centres.

It is possible to be disparaging about this and bemoan, for example, a lost opportunity to settle more residents in central London. But Covent Garden's transformation, whatever its drawbacks, has been a home-grown creation and not one contrived on a drawing board. It is a boisterous success, not to everyone's taste, but it is founded on genuine appetite. In the end, real cities have to be formed like this.

169. *(Above) Restored shopfronts in Shelton Street.*

170. *(Left) The new Tesco Metro store at the corner of Bedford Street and King Street.*

171. A deserted James Street c1968, showing the terrace of market traders' premises that was taken down for the building of the rear extension of the Royal Opera House.

Further Reading

Chancellor, E. Beresford: *The Annals of Covent Garden and its neighbourhood* (1929).

Dane, Clemence: *London has a garden* (1964).

Dent, Alan: *My Covent Garden* (1973).

Dobbs, Brian: *Drury Lane: three centuries of the Theatre Royal 1663-1971* (1972).

Franchi, Francesca and Fryer, Henry: *A history of the Royal Opera House, Covent Garden 1732-1982* (1982).

Gordon, Charles: *Old Time Aldwych, Kingsway and neighbourhood* (1905).

Greater London Council: *Covent Garden's Moving. The Covent Garden Area Draft Plan* (1968).

Greater London Council: *The Next Step. The Revised Plan for the Proposed Comprehensive Development Area* (1971).

Jenkins, Simon: *Landlords to London* (1975).

Long, Marilyn: *Covent Garden and her craftsmen* (1975).

MacMichael, J.H: *The Story of Charing Cross and its immediate neighbourhood* (1906).

Macqueen-Pope, Walter J: *Theatre Royal, Drury Lane* (1945).

Rosenthal, H.D: *Two centuries of opera at Covent Garden* (1958).

Shawe-Taylor, Desmond: *Covent Garden* (1948).

Survey of London Vol. 5: *St Giles in the Fields (part II)* (1914).

Survey of London Vol. 36: *St Paul's Covent Garden* (1970).

Survey of London Vol. 35: *The Theatre Royal Drury Lane and the Royal Opera House, Covent Garden* (1970).

Swinnerton, Frank: *The Bookman's London* (1951).

Thorne, Robert: *Covent Garden Market: its history and restoration* (1980).

Webber, Ron: *Covent Garden: Mud salad market* (1969).

Wyndham, Henry Saxe: *The annals of Covent Garden Theatre, 1732-1897* (1906).

The Illustrations

Most illustrations were supplied by Historical Publications Ltd. The following have kindly given their permission to reproduce illustrations:

London Borough of Camden: *48, 52, 100, 120, 138*
Greater London Record Office: *19, 23, 55, 81, 127, 129, 130, 154, 160, 171*
Peter Jackson Picture Collection: *20*
Messrs Henry Joel & Co: *123*
Metropolitan Police: *92*
Moss Bros: *125*
Messrs J. Sainsbury: *126*
Trustees of Sir John Soane's Museum *20*
City of Westminster: *61, 62, 63, 65, 76, 79, 83, 124, 137, 145, 150, 151, 153, 161*

The proposed plan for Seven Dials (ill. 44) was taken from the Survey of London Vol. 5, *St Giles in the Fields (Pt. II)* (1914).

INDEX
Illustrations are denoted by asterisks